# THE ECONOMICS OF BLACK COMMUNITY DEVELOPMENT

## An Analysis and Program for Autonomous Growth and Development

### FRANK G. DAVIS
*Howard University*

Markham Series in Public Policy Analysis

MARKHAM PUBLISHING COMPANY / Chicago

# MARKHAM SERIES IN PUBLIC POLICY ANALYSIS
Julius Margolis and Aaron Wildavsky, Editors

Bish, *The Public Economy of Metropolitan Areas*

Bogart, ed., *Social Research and the Desegregation of the U.S. Army*

Davis, *The Economics of Black Community Development: An Analysis and Program for Autonomous Growth and Development*

Davis and Dolbeare, *Little Groups of Neighbors: The Selective Service System*

Downs, *Urban Problems and Prospects*

Feldstein, *Economic Analysis for Health Service Efficiency*

Hansen and Weisbrod, *Benefits, Costs, and Finance of Public Higher Education*

Kershaw, *Government Against Poverty*

Leites and Wolf, *Rebellion and Authority: An Analytic Essay on Insurgent Conflicts*

Levy, *Northern Schools and Civil Rights: The Racial Imbalance Act of Massachusetts*

Merewitz and Sosnick, *The Budget's New Clothes: A Critique of Planning-Programming-Budgeting and Benefit-Cost Analysis*

Neenan, *Political Economy of Urban Areas*

Wagner, *The Fiscal Organization of American Federalism*

*Where there is no vision the people perish. . . .*
Proverbs 29:18

# FOREWORD

For many years, black scholars—especially those in economics—have been waiting for a systematic, thorough, and penetrating analysis of the black community from one who possesses the sensitivity and intimate knowledge of its workings and subtleties. Finally, in Frank G. Davis's treatise, *Economics of Black Community Development*, such an analysis is available.

Professor Davis has brought to this work the economist's tools of analysis, but has gone beyond traditional analysis of cost and benefit to inquire into the nature of the process that is black economic development. His laboratory is the overwhelmingly black community of Newark, a prime example of an urban ghetto. His treatment of the many sectors of that community and of the interaction between these sectors and the larger white communities—private and public—represent a major thrust forward in the modern analysis of urban economic development and its unique posture in a black community.

This landmark work should be the beginning of a new era in economic analysis of urban communities and of the development of black peoples. At last a truly representative work, which is the basis of intelligent discussion and researchable findings, has been made available to blacks and to the entire intellectual community. We are all in great debt to Professor Davis for his pioneering effort.

Marcus Alexis
Chairman, Caucus of Black Economists
Professor of Economics and Urban
Affairs, Northwestern University

# PREFACE

Several years ago, my students at Lincoln University (Pennsylvania) began questioning the relevance of economic and intellectual tools to the social and economic problems and issues facing the black ghettos of America. It became quite clear that any initial motivation of black students in economics depended much upon three factors: how relevant economics was to the economic problems of the black ghetto, what could be done to solve those problems, and how they as students could prepare themselves to contribute to a solution.

To meet student demands for an action-oriented economics, the material of this book was prepared and used in manuscript form as a basic text in the economics department and as a basic reference in the social sciences departments.

In the economics department the impact of the material upon student interest in economics has been amazing. The number of majors in economics more than tripled in three years. The students felt that economics had become alive in their lives. They were anxious to learn how a black economist appraised certain crucial issues, such as (1) the present state of affairs of the black community, and how economic forces outside and inside the black ghetto generate and perpetuate poverty and unemployment, (2) how the real income of the black ghettos is falling over time, (3) the ineffectiveness and appropriateness of present and proposed governmental policies in offsetting the falling real income of the black ghetto, and above all (4) how the financial and economic structure of the ghetto could be changed so as to generate autonomous growth and development. In this book I have constructed a program of resource control, including the major constraints upon employment; the ghetto production function; and the growth path of a ghetto economy.

The latter half of the book, the solution to the problem of black community development, has aroused the interest of community leaders as well as college students. It deals with counteracting the tendency toward a fall in the real wage income of ghetto dwellers as a whole, as the national income rises. Some basic questions are:

1. What is the possibility of a more productive role for the black ghetto community as a whole in the economic system?

2. If there is a more productive role, what is it?

3. How can the low rate of income class mobility among ghetto workers employed outside the ghetto be made to generate capital growth within the ghetto?

4. In order to achieve an optimum condition of income flow between black and white communities, what would be the economics of restructuring the ghetto economy so as to optimize the distribution of a rising national income among ghetto residents?

My attempt to find answers to these and other questions in terms of modern economic analysis has been truly an exciting experience. Much of my enthusiasm is due to a feeling that I have discovered through economic analysis the optimum solution, under present conditions, to the problem of black ghetto development. I can only hope that some of my excitement will rub off on those readers who have the power to act.

As to final acknowledgments, I wish to thank Professor William Baumol of Princeton University, Chairman of the (New Jersey) Governor's Economic Policy Council, for the grant I received from the council to study the capital expansion possibilities of the ghetto in Newark, New Jersey. I also thank Professor Baumol for his comments and suggestions. My Lincoln University colleagues deserve my gratitude, especially Firdaus Jhabvala, who rendered invaluable assistance in some of the mathematical aspects. I am grateful for the comments and suggestions of Professor George Borts of Brown University. For reviewing the work and for writing the Foreword, I owe a special dept to my colleague of the Caucus of Black Economists, Professor Marcus Alexis of Northwestern University. I wish to express my special appreciation to Eleanor McConnell of Markham Publishing Company for efficient editorial service. And I must not leave out my wife, Joy, who above all takes full credit for this work.

# CONTENTS

*Part I*

# THE PRESENT STATE
# OF AFFAIRS

# Chapter I

# INTRODUCTION

The persistence of black ghetto poverty,[1] high rates of unemployment of black workers even during periods of prosperity,[2] and the general maladjustment of blacks with respect to the resources of the economy have all led to a great deal of social engineering in the black community.[3] While it is recognized that the obvious need of black ghettos is jobs and income,[4] to this writer's knowledge no economist has yet presented a systematic and integrated analytical

[1] Some recent estimates show that nonwhites enter poverty at more than twice the rate at which whites enter, and the probability of a nonwhite family escaping poverty is about three-fourths that for a white family. In general, almost twice as many families remain poor as become nonpoor. See Terrence F. Kelly, "Factors Affecting Poverty: A Gross Flow Analysis," in President's Commission on Income Maintenance Programs, *Technical Studies* (Washington, D.C.: U.S. Government Printing Office, 1970), pp. 24, 26.

[2] Between 1965 and 1966, when real private gross national product rose 5.6 percent and employment in the privtae economy rose 3.0 percent, the ratio of the nonwhite unemployment rate to the white unemployment rate actually *rose* from 1965 to 1966. This indicates that nonwhites entered poverty at a higher rate than whites and escaped at a slower rate (Kelly, "Factors Affecting Poverty," p. 10).

[3] This consists of a series of economic nostrums to help individual black workers under the cover of OEO and other palliatives, such as "black capitalism" and, more recently, the proposed Income Maintenance Program.

[4] See Charles C. Killingsworth, "Jobs and Income for Negroes," in *Policy Papers in Human Resources and Industrial Relations,* No. 6 (Ann Arbor, Michigan, Institute of Labor and Industrial Relations and the National Manpower Policy Task Force, May, 1968).

approach to the solution of the ghetto development problem. To be sure, there has been much statistical output on the social and economic conditions of Negroes.[5] Nevertheless, the use of these data by economists has followed the conventional wisdom that the poverty of blacks (looked at in terms of black/white income differentials) can be approached in terms of the concept of individual supply and demand analysis for Negro labor,[6] where discrimination is taken to be reflected in both supply and demand forces. In the case of education, for example, educational job standards of quality or quantity make discrimination a supply phenomenon; blacks and whites are supplied different education (in terms of quality or quantity) at the same price.

. In the job market, discrimination is conceived of as a demand phenomenon: two racial groups are demanded at a different price (alternatively, fewer services are demanded from one group than from another at the same price).

This individual supply and demand approach to Negro development places economic analysis in the position of chasing the rainbow of nondiscriminatory markets in a highly complex system of industrial concentration. This raises some fundamental questions: Just what analytical tools should the economist use in approaching the phenomenon of poor blacks? Is the phenomenon of poor blacks different from that of poor whites, except for discrimination? If the answer is yes, does the phenomenon of black ghetto poverty come within the purview of economics by way of the theory of individual supply and demand analysis with all the attendant assumptions of the pure competitive model, modified only by racial barriers? If so, does not the logic of a racially modified competitive model lead to the view that the black ghetto is merely a residential area, similar to any other residential area, even white suburbia, except that the individual inhabitants of the ghetto happen to be black and also happen to be poor because of the unfortunate circumstances of present racial discrimination? Does the logic of such a competitive

[5] For more recent and comprehensive data, see The President's Commission on Income Maintenance Programs, *Technical Studies* and *Background Papers by the Commission* (Washington, D.C.: U.S. Government Printing Office, 1970).

[6] Kelly, "Factors Affecting Poverty," p. 32.

model, adjusted for racial factors, constitute a fruitful economic abstraction in analyzing the incidence of poverty among black people, and in planning the future course for their economic development? My answer is no. My basic hypothesis is that the economic forces generating black poverty are different[7] from those that generate white poverty. In this respect black poverty differs from white poverty, notwithstanding racial discrimination in the job market.

## THE OBJECTIVE OF THIS BOOK

The basic analytical objective is to examine, within the prevailing economic and social structure of the American economy, the optimum economic relationship between the black ghetto economy and the general economy. The ghetto economy is viewed as predominantly labor intensive; the general economy is viewed as highly oligopolistic and capital intensive and as becoming increasingly more capital intensive through automation. This automation, when combined with oligopoly, will undoubtedly: (1) lessen the aggregate demand at any given time for blue collar production workers, both black and white, in high productivity manufacturing industries; (2) weaken maintainable consumer demand and the growth prospects of urban communities; and (3) continue to generate income inequality within the system as a whole and to impose external diseconomies upon the utilization of resources within the black ghettos.

In Part I we will analyze the present state of affairs of the black community, including the following steps:

1. Demonstrate that the conventional approach to the problem of black community development—by means of a microeconomic model of supply and demand analysis within racial constraints—sheds no light on the problem of black community development but leads only to a point of supply and demand equilibrium in the

[7] Alan Batchelder, "Poverty: The Special Case of the Negro," *American Economic Review, Papers and Proceedings* 2 (May, 1965), p. 530. In this paper, Batchelder identified five economic considerations that distinguished Negro poverty from white poverty.

Negro job market, short of full employment, at a wage rate that yields incomes below the poverty level.

2. Explain the aspirations and goals of the black community.

3. Test a new agenda of hypotheses on the utilization of black labor in terms of certain exogenous factors that restrict the economic development of the black ghetto economy.

4. Analyze the ghetto market system and economic structure empirically.

5. Analyze the problem of ghetto development in terms of factors endogenous to the ghetto community as a subeconomy rather than as a residential area.

In Part II we will consider the effects of present and proposed governmental policies upon ghetto development. In Part III we will show the economic implications of our hypotheses, with respect to factors exogenous to the ghetto economy as well as endogenous factors, in terms of a solution to the problem of ghetto development.

## THE CONVENTIONAL APPROACH TO GHETTO DEVELOPMENT

Conventional approaches to ghetto development are mainly in terms of the microeconomic model of supply and demand analysis. Discrimination on both the supply and demand side is taken to represent the major impediment to black community development.

### The Demand Phenomenon of Discrimination

In analyzing the demand phenomenon of discrimination, economists such as Gwartney[8] have undertaken to measure discrimination (on the demand side) by adjusting for differences in income in terms of productivity factors (quantity of education, level of scholastic achievement, regional, age, and city-size distributions). It has been concluded by Gwartney that "while the unadjusted income of nonwhites was only 58.3 percent as great as whites, the income of non-

[8] James Gwartney, "Discrimination and Income Differentials," *American Economic Review, Papers and Proceedings* 3 (June, 1970), p. 396.

white urban males is estimated between 81 and 87 percent of white income after adjustment for the five factors of productivity. An income between 13 and 19 percent remains unexplained." Gwartney attributes this residual largely to discrimination.

Two major difficulties are inherent in this view of black/white income differentials in terms of discrimination in the job market, even after adjusting for productivity factors. The first difficulty is methodological; the other stems from underlying assumptions implicit in the black/white income analysis. Methodologically, summary measures, such as black/white median income, are quite misleading if the attempt is to measure (at least by implication) the relative well-being of blacks compared with whites, if there were no discrimination. Data on black median income as a percentage of white median income do not really measure changes in ghetto poverty (with or without discrimination) because factors that affect ghetto poverty are different from factors that alter the income level of higher income blacks. For example, inflation leads to more unequal black incomes.[9] That is, there is greater income dispersion.[10] This occurs because the bulk of ghetto residents are low-paid unskilled workers, experiencing high rates of unemployment, and receiving limited raises above the legal minimum wage during periods of inflation—as will be shown later. Thus, the impact of factors such as inflation has one effect upon the median income of blacks as a whole, quite a different effect upon the fixed incomes (legal minimum) of a large mass of unskilled ghetto labor, and yet a different effect on higher-income blacks.

The underlying assumptions of the demand phenomenon of market discrimination are that over time the demand for black ghetto labor will be made to shift upward to the right if job discrimination is somehow eliminated. This assumption, however, is not applicable to the large mass of unskilled ghetto labor where unemployment rates are high, come boom or depression. For example, unemployment rates of 20 percent among adult Negro men in cen-

[9] Lester C. Thurow, "Analyzing the American Income Distribution," *American Economic Review, Papers and Proceedings* 2 (May, 1970), p. 262.

[10] Thurow, "Analyzing the American Income Distribution," p. 262. Thurow reports that the income distribution for blacks is much more widely dispersed than for whites. The Gini Coefficient for blacks is substantially higher than it is for whites.

tral city ghettos of six large cities[11] during 1968 and 1969 could hardly be directly attributable to individual employer discrimination. Thus, the poverty results of this inordinate unemployment rate in central city ghettos appear to be only indirectly related to individual employer discrimination, at least on the demand side. This suggests that perhaps a growing number of these unskilled workers are redundant to the requirements for unskilled labor in manufacturing industries where technological changes are occurring. If this is so, the demand for unskilled black labor in high-paying industry will shift downward, will do so cumulatively, and will become quite large over time. The result, of course, will be a perpetuation of low wages and poverty in the black ghetto, together with a continuous rise, during periods of prosperity, in income inequality between lower-income ghetto blacks and higher-income nonghetto blacks. In this case, changes over time in the overall income differentials between black and white may have little or no effect upon the poverty of unskilled ghetto blacks.

## The Supply Phenomenon of Discrimination

With respect to education as a major factor on the supply side, some economists have approached the problem of personal income distribution in terms of the rate of returns on "varied mixtures of human resources." [12] The objective is to determine the rate of return on training as an investment in human capital (raw labor). Thomas Johnson[13] has developed a model that will predict lifetime earnings. The model is "formulated such that parameters can be estimated simultaneously and hypotheses tested for several types of investment in human capital, as a function of race and region."

If we assume that employer demand for blacks is a function of the relative rates of return on educating and training blacks, com-

[11] Atlanta, Chicago, Detroit, Houston, Los Angeles, and New York. This was the case at any time during the year July 1968 to June 1969. U.S. Department of Labor, Bureau of Labor Statistics, *Report No. 375;* and U.S. Department of Commerce, Bureau of the Census, *Current Population Reports,* Series P-23, No. 29 (Washington, D.C.: U.S. Government Printing Office, 1970), p. 93.

[12] Gary S. Becker, *The Economics of Discrimination* (Chicago: University of Chicago Press, 1957).

[13] Thomas Johnson, "Returns from Investment in Human Capital," *American Economic Review* 4 (September, 1970), p. 546.

pared with rates on whites, we may test the validity of this hypothesis by observing the level of investment in the education and training of blacks where the rate of returns on educating and training blacks is higher than for whites. This hypothesis implies that the employer follows the profit motive and will hire blacks if the supply costs of on-the-job training (OJT) are less than for whites.

In testing this hypothesis, my analysis of Johnson's data and computations reveals the following conclusions: (1) At all levels of schooling, net schooling investment for blacks is substantially less than for whites in both the North and the South. (2) At all levels of schooling, total lifetime earnings of whites rise progressively and significantly up through graduate school, while lifetime earnings of blacks reach a peak for those whose schooling is between the ninth and twelfth grades and fall thereafter until a year of graduate work is completed.

For a given unit of supply of raw black labor seeking schooling as an investment, the data show that it does not pay (in terms of observed life earnings) for the individual black to go beyond the ninth grade unless he plans to complete college and go to graduate school. Except for the black who goes to graduate school, the total observed income from the end of schooling until retirement (at age 65) is maximized, beginning with schooling at the eighth or ninth grade level. His maximized lifetime earnings at the ninth grade level are $155,000 in the North and $101,437 in the South, and these earnings stay within the range of schooling between the ninth and twelfth grades. After the twelfth grade, further investment in education among blacks is accompanied by a fall in total earnings between school and retirement, until the graduate level is reached. Since the lifetime earnings of the black worker go down with additional schooling beyond the twelfth grade, the black worker earns his highest rate of return on his investment in education with schooling between the ninth and twelfth grades.

On the basis of these data, we can observe that (except for graduate work) it pays the black worker to drop out of high school and take low-paying jobs,[14] in terms of both his total lifetime earnings and the rate of return on his investment in education. This implies

[14] Jobs that pay below the poverty level. Lifetime earnings of $155,000, starting at age 16 and ending at age 65, would yield average annual earnings below the poverty level for a family of four.

that the supply schedule for the individual black is infinitely elastic at some low wage rate that maximizes his rate of return on his investment in education. From the employers' side (demand for labor) we can observe that at all levels of schooling from the fifth grade upward the employer pays the individual black substantially less than he pays the individual white. Also, at all levels of schooling, the gross on-the-job training (OJT) investment in blacks is substantially less than gross OJT investment for whites. In other words, the employer pays the individual black less than he pays the individual white and invests less in the black's OJT. This implies that both the employer's schedule of demand for black labor and his schedule of investment in blacks are quite different from his schedules for white labor. In this separate black labor market, the point of equilibrium between (1) the employer's demand schedule for black labor at lower levels of OJT and rates of pay, and (2) the black worker's supply schedule in terms of the wage rate that will maximize the rate of return on his education over his working life is the crucial question. As previously mentioned, the supply schedule of the individual black worker is logically infinitely elastic at some wage rate that will maximize his total lifetime earnings and yield the highest rate of return on his schooling investment. What, then, is the employer willing to do at the point where his demand schedule is assumed to cut an infinitely elastic labor supply schedule? The answer is shown in Table 1-1.

Observe that the quantities in Table 1-1 representing non-white/North and white/North[15] indicate that a schooling level (9–11 to 12) where the rate of return on educating blacks (.3926) is highest, net positive OJT investment[16] is lowest, and net OJT is negative by $402. Also, any value above or below –$402 gives a larger negative net positive OJT investment or a larger net positive OJT investment. Beyond this equilibrium point of supply and demand for black labor, which occurs at a low wage rate, the employer prefers investing in white labor whose total lifetime earnings rise for those with some college training (12 to 13–15 years of schooling)

---

[15] Quantities for nonwhite and white South differ mostly in the order of magnitude of the quantities (lower) but show generally the same relationship between nonwhite and white.

[16] Net positive on-the-job training (OJT) investment is defined as the integral of net OJT investment from the end of schooling to the time at which net investment is zero.

Table 1-1.   Quantities Derived from Parameter Estimates

| Race, region | Lower level school- ing | Upper level school- ing | Rate of return | Gross OJT invest- ment | Net positive invest- ment | Net positive OJT invest- ment | Total lifetime earnings (to age 65) |
|---|---|---|---|---|---|---|---|
| Nonwhite, north | 8 | 9–11 | .3187 | $28,359 | $1,671 | $ 7,322 | $138,410 |
| | 8 | 12 | .2841 | 33,442 | −1,392 | 6,857 | 155,129 |
| | 9–11 | 12 | .3926 | 24,286 | −402 | 5,158 | 155,092 |
| | 12 | 13–15 | .1747 | 46,396 | −6,406 | 6,793 | 146,937 |
| White, north | 8 | 9–11 | .2456 | $68,335 | $ 902 | $15,316 | $220,025 |
| | 8 | 12 | .2146 | 67,664 | −690 | 14,704 | 245,433 |
| | 9–11 | 12 | .2521 | 57,951 | 453 | 13,235 | 245,399 |
| | 12 | 13–15 | .1752 | 93,916 | −6,598 | 17,170 | 278,323 |

Source: Thomas Johnson, "Returns from Investment in Human Capital," *American Economic Review* 4 (September, 1970), p. 558.

while the total lifetime earnings of blacks with some college training fall.

We conclude that the competitive model of individual supply and demand analysis where discrimination is assumed to be reflected on both the supply and demand side does not shed any light on why rates of unemployment are high among black workers where the individual, when employed, can maximize the rate of return on his education at low wage levels. The model does help us to see that (on the supply side) the supply curve of the individual black laborer is probably infinitely elastic at some low wage where the rate of return on his education is maximized when schooling is between ninth and twelfth grades. At this low poverty wage, returns on educating and training the individual black are higher than for individual whites. But this microobservation does not help us approach the poverty problem, especially when the individual employer finds it most profitable to hire and train the individual black worker just at the point where the worker's rate of return on education is highest. This condition of equilibrium at a low wage suggests that it is profitable to both the individual black worker and the individual employer to perpetuate low wages and poverty. That is, if the black individual worker seeks more education, he will forfeit a part of his lifetime earnings, and if the individual employer hires a black with above average education, his net positive OJT investment will rise. His net positive OJT will also rise if he hires a white worker with above average education. Apparently, the employer thinks it is more profitable in the long run to invest in the white worker because there are no racial barriers to his upward mobility in the firm. The competitive model assumes, of course, that the individual employer will not make unprofitable investments even if the law says he must not discriminate in the hiring and training of blacks.

We conclude here that the microeconomic approach to the training and employment of the individual black worker results in a condition of supply and demand equilibrium in the Negro job market when wage rates are below the poverty level. It leaves high rates of unemployment in central city ghettos unaccounted for—except to say that the employer finds it unprofitable in the long run to invest in blacks beyond a point of supply and demand equilibrium at some low wage.

## THE BLACK COMMUNITY'S DESIRE FOR AUTONOMY

The black community as a whole has observed that (1) economic forces, whether in periods of prosperity or depression, generate within the black community both unemployment and underemployment, and (2) post-World War II prosperity has compounded the black community's unemployment and low paying jobs with rising prices and inflation.

As shown in Figure 1-1, the national unemployment rate for black people is about double the unemployment rate for white people in good times and bad times. In periods of recession (1949, 1953–54, 1960–61) Negro unemployment rates rise inordinately, and in periods of expansion Negro unemployment rates remain at what would be called depression rates for the economy as a whole.

Figure 1-2 illustrates Labor Department reports that the unemployment rate in poverty districts during the second quarter of 1969 was 5.7 percent, unchanged over the year. Negro unemployment rates in the poverty areas actually rose from 7.3 to 8 percent during the second quarter of 1969. For the economy as a whole, the ratio

Figure 1-1.  Unemployment Rates by Color, 1948–69,
Annual Third Quarter 1965 Average

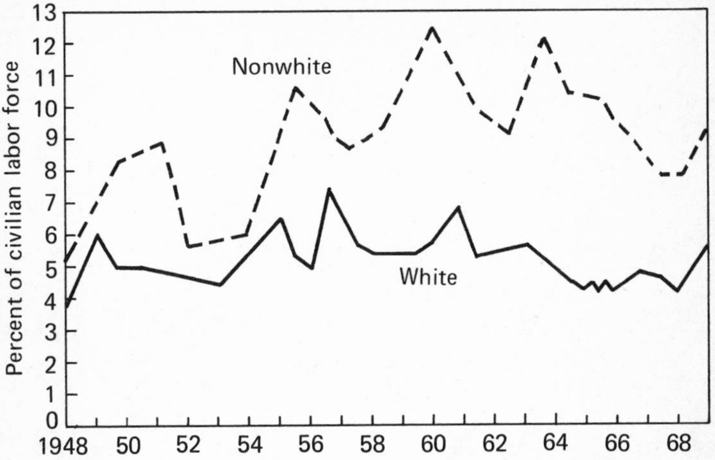

Source: U.S. Dept. of Labor, *The Social and Economic Status of Negroes in the United States* (Washington, D.C.: U.S. Government Printing Office, 1969).

of black to white unemployment was about 2 to 1 during the second quarter of 1969. The ratios move together except in two periods: 1959–60 and 1962–63.

With relatively fixed money wage rates for unskilled black workers in urban ghettos and high levels of employment within the economy as a whole, maximal growth accompanied by rising wage rates and inflationary price rises results in a high rate of Negro unemployment together with drastic reductions in the real income of the black community. This is shown in Figure 1-2, where two separate Phillips curves are drawn out roughly approximating the state of affairs. The one on the left is the national relationship between relative changes in wage rates and unemployment levels. The one on the right presents the picture for the black community.

Figure 1-3 shows the change in consumer prices over the period 1952–69. In aggregate terms, as total output and employment expand under conditions of wage-price push, the persistently high rate of Negro unemployment and low money wage rates result in a constant maintenance of unequal shares of the aggregate output

Figure 1-2.  Effect of Wage Changes on Unemployment

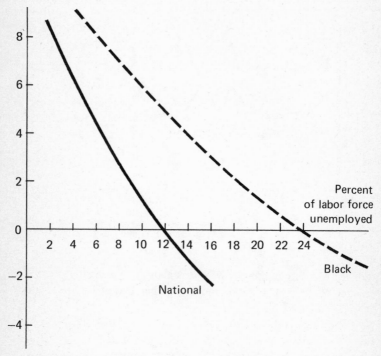

*Note:* Solid line indicates national rates; broken line indicates rates for black population.

going to the black community. And a decrease in the level of employment in the economy as a whole, accompanied by a curtailment of rising prices, leaves the black community with inordinately high and politically unacceptable unemployment rates. Insofar as the politics of black power is concerned, the theory of the trade-off between inflation and unemployment is a theory of choice between the devil of rising poverty and the deep sea of rising unemployment.

Figure 1-3.   Consumer Price Index, All Items, for Selected Years, 1953 to July, 1969

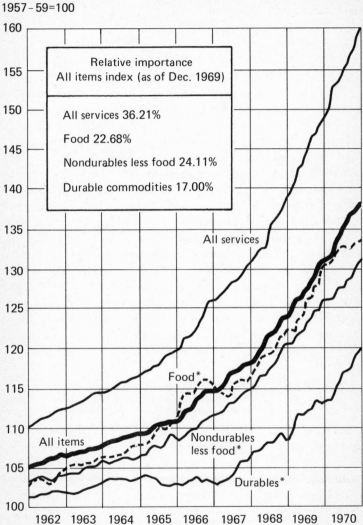

1957 – 59=100

*Seasonally adjusted. Latest data December, 1970.

*Source:* U.S. Dept. of Labor, Bureau of Labor Statistics, December, 1970.

The obvious result of this indifference of the forces of prosperity and depression to the economic plight of the black community has been a continuous increase in the number of black people on relief rolls. For example, the relief rolls of New York City, comprising mostly black people, are expected soon to cost $1 billion annually. The general case of poverty and welfare payments among nonwhite and white is shown in Table 1-2, below.

This steady trend of unemployment, relief, and low wages stands as prima facie evidence of the reasons for the disenchantment of the black community with so-called civil rights legislation and integration. The basic problem confronting the black community becomes the organizational structure of the white economy and the economic forces generated by the structure.

Technological changes in nonagricultural industries under conditions of oligopoly do not result in lower prices and rising demand for black labor. Also, due to agricultural price support, technological changes in agriculture have been accompanied by rising food prices along with the disemployment of black farm workers. In a sense, one may say that the black worker has been kicked off the farm by his former plantation employer and then taxed by the government (via agricultural price support and subsidy) to maintain the prosperity of his former employer. The economic forces vis-à-vis the black community are technological change, rising prices, low wages, unemployment, and underemployment.

Table 1-2. Number and Percent of Persons Below the Poverty Level and of Persons Receiving Welfare, 1966
(Numbers in millions)

|  | Nonwhite | White |
|---|---|---|
| Total population | 23.2 | 170.2 |
| Below poverty level | 9.6 | 20.1 |
| Percent of total population | 41.0 | 12.0 |
| Receiving welfare | 3.2 | 4.5 |
| Percent of total population | 14.0 | 3.0 |

Source: U.S. Dept. of Health, Education and Welfare, in Social and Economic Conditions of Negroes in the United States, Joint publication, U.S. Dept. of Labor and U.S. Dept. of Commerce (Washington, D.C.: U.S. Government Printing Office, October, 1967), p. 25.

The impact of these economic forces has clearly indicated that civil rights legislation does not necessarily involve basic economic changes in the opportunities for the residents of the black community. In other words, civil rights and civil liberties may be quite independent of the system of resource organization. Ideally, political democracy implies or may imply economic democracy. But the realization of economic democracy may imply a host of assumptions governing the way the economic system works, and many of these assumptions may not conform to the reality of the system. For example, the assumption of free mobility of labor may be a political reality in the sense that there are no legal restrictions on any individual working in any occupation, any industry, or any part of the country, but the economic reality of free mobility of labor may be such that labor may have geographic mobility but not economic mobility. That is, Negroes may be able to move from a declining region of the country, or from a declining industry, but good jobs may not be available once the geographic movement has taken place. The result of this geographic mobility may merely mean a high concentration of labor in a so-called growth region but without employment opportunities in the growing region. So one observes a growing proportion of black people concentrated in urban areas in large cities who persistently are subject to a chronic condition of unemployment[17] and low wages. Workers under such circumstances then would obviously become worse off even with so-called civil rights legislation and integration.

In response to these conditions in the black community, politicians may say that too many promises were made. But reality suggests that political promises governing integration and civil rights are quite distinct from the impact of economic forces governing the utilization and allocation of labor in our economy. It soon becomes clear that political promises, whether prolific or scant, are really irrelevant to economic forces. Or perhaps we should say that economic forces are beyond the reach of political promises. These economic

[17] If the present pace of Negro employment continues, the unemployment rate of Negroes will be five times that of the white population by 1979. Speech by Arthur A. Fletcher, Under Secretary of Labor, at the West Coast Regional Meeting of the NAACP, Asilomar, California (September 20, 1969).

forces, such as oligopoly, industrial concentration, rising prices in the face of technological changes, pervade the American economy and are beyond the pale insofar as politicians are concerned. And any realistic changes in terms of the impact of these forces upon the black community would either require some serious modifications in the economic system as a whole or some serious modification in the allocation of resources within the black community.

Therefore, for the ghetto's man in the street, the concept of integration becomes as "sounding brass and tinkling cymbals," signifying nothing in terms of his economic position. And since the black man knows that he cannot change the way the system as a whole operates, he feels that the next best thing is to control the way the ghetto economy operates. Perhaps he sees this as his only realistic alternative opportunity. After listening to the spokesman of the separate state idea for blacks, he realizes that although the idea of a separate state is appealing, no one has been able to develop an acceptable blueprint. In the meantime he knows that he is already occupying important economic, geographic, and political space in the core of central city and is inclined to do as Booker T. Washington long ago admonished: "let down your buckets where you are." In ghetto lingo, the expression may be interpreted as doing your own thing, being your own man, running your own schools, having your own businesses, and controlling your own community. Viewed politically, this concept of doing your own thing and being your own proud black man appears to be a rejection of racial integration. It really is not; it is more a recognition that racial integration has come too late and is now irrelevant to the problem of chronic unemployment and low wages of the unskilled masses in urban ghettos. The main forces to be dealt with now are technological and economic factors that will, notwithstanding racial integration, continue to adversely affect the economic status of the redundant supply of unskilled workers residing in the ghetto. Further, it is within the framework of these technological and economic forces that the problems of the ghetto must be solved. Therefore, what seems to be a rejection of racial integration is really a rejection of an illusory and irrelevant approach to the problems of the black ghetto. The basic idea is to control and reorganize the resources of the ghetto in terms of the economic forces of technology, unemployment, low wages, and rising prices.

## THE CONTENT OF BLACK POWER

The ideology of free enterprise under conditions of industrial concentration and rapid technological change tends to gloss over the economic difficulties of black people who are oppressed as a group. This is so because the focus of attention is always on the individual and his individual initiative. Under these circumstances, one is always pointing to individual Negroes who have made it, as if to say, if Ralph Bunche can, so can the others. This is, of course, a fallacy of composition. Even more, it creates the illusion of progress for Negroes. When we look at the Negro group as a whole, however, we find that almost three-fourths of all Negro families are in metropolitan areas where almost 60 percent of all Negroes below the poverty level live; while half of all the Negro families in the United States are making less than $5,359 a year, and 29 percent of all Negro families are below the poverty level. This can hardly be construed as economic progress in an economy where the per capita income is about $4,900 compared with the Negro per capita income of approximately $1,632.

In view of the economic and social plight of the Negro in the United States, the ideology of economic individualism is no longer acceptable by the black power movement as a social instrument of black community development. While there will always be a relatively small percentage of Negroes who will make it, the great bulk of Negroes will remain in poverty. The alternatives to the difficulties of individual initiative is some form of group action or group power as a substitute for the failure of individual action. For the black man in the ghetto, group power and group control within the ghetto have become the second best alternative.

### Psychological Elements

The psychological basis for black power emanates from a common set of experiences of the group and a common mode of group behavior with respect to these experiences. The most all-pervasive experience of black people in America has been the difficulty of survival under a set of socially proscribed rules that relegated black people to marginal jobs and marginal economic opportunities. It is only natural that this type of experience generated a psychological defense mechanism known as "Uncle Tomism." Now, the black group as a whole has sensed that the individualistic and personalistic approach of "Uncle Tomism" is no longer the key to group survival. The black man has observed that he is living in a system of power blocs and social grouping, the most pervasive of which is the white establishment, including the white middle class and big business. Thus, his defense mechanism for survival is shifting from the personalistic approach of "Uncle Tomism" to the group approach of black power, a major element of which is group power for survival in a social system of racial grouping and power blocs. The underlying psychology of this black power approach is the concept of black awareness and black identity. This is the psychological and cohesive element that is rooted in the black experience and designed as the mainspring for group action and group recognition.

### Economic Elements

If the psychology of black awareness is group solidarity, the economics of black awareness is group capitalization upon its own resources. Its resources consist mainly of the aggregate purchasing power[18] of the group in a market that has been delineated as the Negro market. This market has certain basic and unique characteristics, to be discussed in a later chapter. In any case, the main attributes of this market have been generated by racial segregation, which defines its spatial dimensions as well as its psychological characteristics in terms of the patterns of Negro consumer choices. A major economic element of black power, therefore, is group control of and group benefit from its own market potential. To the extent that this is possible, both the economic and political power of the group would be greater. Greater bargaining power would accrue to black workers because of alternative opportunities for employment either within or outside the ghetto.

## A VIEW OF BLACK COMMUNITY POVERTY

While social scientists recognize that a serious income and employment gap exists between white and black Americans, there is a

[18] Estimated at $36.4 billion for 1969.

general tendency to apply personalistic blame to the Negro for the fatherless family, to the high rate of school dropouts, or to the lack of education. The outstanding exception to this tendency is found in the *Kerner Report,* which points to white racism as the blame. Curiously, no one has taken an objective or scientific view about the way the economic system operates either within or outside the ghetto. No one has yet inquired whether the basic economic structure of the ghetto generates poverty, or whether economic growth within the economy generates greater income inequality between the black ghetto and the rest of the economy, notwithstanding school dropouts, white racism, or fatherless black families.

The failure to take a scientific approach concerning the organization of ghetto resources and the impact of general economic changes upon the growth of ghetto poverty rules out any real understanding of the problem of the black community, or the goals of the black community, or the full meaning of the black power concept.

The failure to understand the problems and goals of the black community has resulted in a series of economic nostrums to help individual black workers under the cover of the Office of Economic Opportunity (OEO) and other economic palliatives, now called black capitalism, designed to help individual black businessmen.

# Chapter 2

# THE PROBLEM AND A NEW AGENDA OF HYPOTHESES

In the light of the goals of the black community, let us now consider some alternative hypotheses with respect to the problem of utilizing a large mass of unemployed, unskilled black labor residing in the central city ghettos. Here the approach to black economic development is mainly macroeconomic, to focus upon the functioning of the market system as a whole vis-à-vis the utilization of the labor resources of the black population.

In this connection, we drop the competitive individual supply and demand model in which discrimination is taken to be reflected in both supply and demand forces and the objective of public policy is (1) to track down individual employer discrimination and (2) to seek to educate and train individual blacks to take jobs with apparently nondiscriminatory individual employers. We will take discrimination as given, systemic and ineradicable in the market system as a whole, and certainly ineradicable on an employer-by-employer basis.

## THE GENERAL NATURE OF THE BLACK DEVELOPMENT PROBLEM

Our point of departure is that the black economic development problem is the central problem of urban development. Poverty and

Table 2-1.   Percentage Distribution of Nonwhite Families and
Percentage Below Poverty Level, 1965

| Area | Distribution of nonwhite families (percent) | Nonwhite families in each location below the poverty level (percent) |
|---|---|---|
| United States | 100 | 39 |
| Farm | 5 | 68 |
| Nonfarm | 95 | 35 |
| Small town rural area | 21 | 56 |
| Metropolitan area | 74 | 30 |
| 1,000,000 or more | 45 | 25 |
| 250,000 to 1,000,000 | 21 | 34 |
| Under 250,000 | 8 | 41 |

Sources: U.S. Dept. of Commerce, Bureau of the Census, *Current Population Reports,* Series P-23, No. 24 and U.S. Dept. of Labor, Bureau of Labor Statistics, *BLS Report* No. 332.

property deterioration are greatest in the urban slums inhabited mostly by blacks. The rebuilding of the slums is a necessary but not a sufficient condition of urban economic development. Urban economic development is entwined with the problem of poverty and the efficient utilization of a growing proportion of black workers in the central city of metropolitan areas where over half of all Negro families live.[1] Also, urban renewal will not eliminate the problem of poverty and efficient utilization of Negro labor.

Some indication of the magnitude of the problem is shown in Table 2-1 by the location of all nonwhite families in 1965 and the percentage of those below the poverty level in each location. It will be noted that in the large metropolitan areas (1 million population or more) where 45 percent of nonwhite families live, one-fourth of such families were below the poverty level. This large percentage of poor families suggests that the general nature of the problem of Negro development is to counteract the economic forces outside and within the ghetto that generate poverty by restricting full and efficient utilization of black labor. Outside the ghetto, the economic forces that impinge upon the ghetto are mainly rapid technological changes under conditions of oligopoly. Within the ghetto these

[1] Fifty-four percent in 1968. The number of Negroes in central cities rose from 9.5 million in 1960 to 11.9 million in 1968.

economic forces are generated mainly by the enclave nature of the ghetto economic structure.

## EFFECTS OF EXOGENOUS FORCES

The outside forces that generate poverty in central city ghettos consist mainly of rapid technological changes in manufacturing under conditions of oligopolistic pricing. These forces generate poverty in at least eight ways:

1. Expansion of investment in manufacturing industries depends heavily upon technological changes that lower production costs.

2. Under oligopoly pricing, the price level is rigid (downward) but shows remarkable upward flexibility.

3. Technological changes in manufacturing, together with a condition of oligopolistic price maintenance, reduce the demand in manufacturing for black ghetto labor, which is predominantly un-skilled, and the supply of black labor as a whole becomes redundant to high productivity and high paying manufacturing industries.

4. The redundant supply of unskilled black labor no longer needed in manufacturing[2] must compete for jobs in low productivity employment and low paying service industries where black workers are already concentrated.

5. Low paying trade and service industries with fixed labor/capital ratios can expand during periods of prosperity without raising the real wages of unskilled labor substantially above the real wage equivalent of the legal money wage for unskilled workers.

6. The operation of economic forces within the economy is such that the black ghettoes become worse off as total output expands, and the crucial political issue of the black community is *group sur-vival in a sea of economic forces with strong undercurrents of racism.* This is shown in Table 2-2. Industrial output rose by 51.8 percent between 1959 and 1967 and the real income of ghetto workers fell by 0.6 percent over the period.

[2] Alan Batchelder, "Poverty: The Special Case of the Negro," *American Economic Review* 2 (May, 1965), p. 536.

Table 2-2.  Comparison of Changes in Industrial
Output with Changes in Real Wages of Ghetto
Workers, 1959 and 1967

| Year | Index of industrial production (1957–59 = 100) | Percent change in ghetto worker real wages, 1959–67 (in 1957–59 prices) |
|---|---|---|
| 1959 | 106.0 | 100.0 |
| 1967 | 157.8 | 99.4 |

Sources: Board of Governors of Federal Reserve
System, "Industrial Production, 1957–59 Base," in Edwin
B. Cox, *Basic Tables in Business and Economics* (New
York: McGraw-Hill Book Co., 1967), p. 319; and U.S.
Dept. of Commerce, *Trends in Social and Economic Conditions of Negroes in Metropolitan Areas* (Washington,
D.C.: U.S. Government Printing Office, 1969).

7. The economic problem of low productivity jobs and industries, where ghetto labor is overrepresented, is beyond the reach of monetary and fiscal policies, whether under conditions of prosperity or recession. Under both sets of conditions, the black ghettos will show high rates of unemployment and low wages. In these low productivity jobs, a high proportion of black workers employed therein earned less than $3,000 in 1966. This is shown in Table 2-3.

It is observed from Table 2-3 that in trade and service industries, 36 percent and 25 percent, respectively, of black men were employed at a wage below $3,000 compared with 16 percent in manufacturing.

Table 2-3.  Comparison of White and Nonwhite Workers According
to the Number and Percent of Low Earners,
by Selected Industries, 1966

| Industry | Number of white low earners (in thousands) | As percent of all whites employed | Number of nonwhite low earners (in thousands) | As percent of all nonwhites employed |
|---|---|---|---|---|
| Construction | 111 | 5 | 53 | 27 |
| Manufacturing | 348 | 3 | 160 | 16 |
| Trade | 300 | 7 | 160 | 36 |
| Service industries | 322 | 7 | 147 | 25 |

Source: U.S. Dept. of Labor, *Manpower Report of the President* (Washington,
D.C.: U.S. Government Printing Office, 1968), p. 33.

Table 2-4.  Percentage Distribution of Employment of Nonwhite
Workers and Index of Change in Employment by Broad Occupation
Groups, 1954–65

| Year | Agriculture Per-cent | Agriculture Index 1954 = 100 | Blue collar Per-cent | Blue collar Index 1954 = 100 | White collar Per-cent | White collar Index 1954 = 100 | Service Per-cent | Service Index 1954 = 100 |
|---|---|---|---|---|---|---|---|---|
| 1954 | 15.5 | 100.0 | 41.8 | 100.0 | 11.8 | 100.0 | 30.8 | 100.0 |
| 1955 | 14.5 | 93.5 | 42.0 | 100.4 | 12.0 | 101.6 | 31.6 | 102.5 |
| 1956 | 14.5 | 93.5 | 41.7 | 99.7 | 11.5 | 97.4 | 32.2 | 104.5 |
| 1957 | 13.8 | 89.0 | 41.4 | 99.0 | 12.8 | 108.4 | 32.0 | 103.8 |
| 1958 | 12.7 | 81.9 | 40.5 | 96.8 | 13.7 | 116.1 | 33.1 | 107.4 |
| 1959 | 12.9 | 83.2 | 40.9 | 97.8 | 14.7 | 124.5 | 31.9 | 103.5 |
| 1960 | 12.4 | 80.0 | 39.8 | 95.2 | 16.0 | 135.5 | 31.8 | 103.2 |
| 1961 | 11.7 | 75.4 | 39.1 | 93.5 | 16.4 | 138.9 | 33.2 | 107.7 |
| 1962 | 11.0 | 70.9 | 39.5 | 94.4 | 16.7 | 141.5 | 32.8 | 106.4 |
| 1963 | 9.7 | 62.5 | 39.8 | 95.2 | 17.7 | 150.0 | 32.8 | 106.4 |
| 1964 | 8.7 | 56.1 | 40.3 | 96.4 | 18.7 | 158.4 | 32.2 | 104.5 |
| 1965 | 8.1 | 52.2 | 40.7 | 97.3 | 19.5 | 165.2 | 31.7 | 102.9 |

Source: U.S. Dept. of Labor, *The Negroes in the United States, Their Economic
and Social Situations*. Bulletin No. 1511 (Washington, D.C.: U.S. Government Printing Office, June, 1966).

The impact of economic forces upon the industrial affiliation of
black workers in high-paying and high-productivity blue collar
employment is shown in Table 2-4 below.

It will be observed that while the downward trend in the proportion of black workers in agriculture has been most dramatic between 1954 and 1965 there has been also a steady, though less
dramatic, downward trend in the proportion of all black workers
in blue collar employment. Along with this trend, we observe in
these blue collar jobs that blacks are heavily concentrated in the
lowest-paid categories.[3]

The relatively smaller decline between 1954 and 1965 in the proportion of all black workers in blue collar production work, along
with their continuous concentration in the lowest-paid categories of
a blue collar employment, has a much greater economic significance

---

[3] Office of Research and Reports, Equal Employment Opportunity Commission, *Nine City Group Employment Profile,* Research Report 1967-19-A,
August 6, 1967.

than appears on the surface. It means a *reversal* of a possible shift of unskilled black labor from lower-paid service and blue collar employment where black workers in general are over-represented, to higher-paying industrial jobs where black workers are under-represented. The trend of employment of black workers, however, is toward further concentration in industries with the highest proportions of low-wage black workers. This is shown in Table 2-5, where it is observed that between 1960 and 1969 Negroes employed in service-production industries rose to over two-fifths of their total employment while those employed as semiskilled rose to roughly one-fourth. Those employed as skilled (craftsmen) increased from 7.4 percent to 8.4 percent, representing a 1 percent increase over a nine-year period.

The nature and scope of the imbalance in the industrial affiliations of black workers, which are now being affected adversely by technological trends, are shown in Table 2-6.

It is observed, for example, that in 1964 the percent of male nonwhite of total male was 22.9 percent in hospital work as compared with only 4.8 percent in electrical machinery, 19.4 percent in personal service as compared with 7.8 percent in manufacturing.

The reversal of the possibility of the movement of unskilled black labor into higher-paying production work in manufacturing is, of course, a reflection of a general change in the industrial distribution of civilian employment. This is shown in Figure 2-1, which

Table 2-5. Changes in the Proportion of Total Negroes Employed, by Selected Occupations, 1960–69

|  | 1960 | 1969 |
| --- | --- | --- |
| Total employed Negroes[a] | 6,927 | 8,369 |
| Number in service producing industry | 1,918 | 2,766 |
| Percent of total employed | 27.7 | 41.5 |
| Number employed as semiskilled[b] | 1,414 | 1,998 |
| Percent of total employed | 20.4 | 23.9 |
| Number employed as skilled | 515 | 704 |
| Percent of total employed | 7.4 | 8.4 |

[a] Includes Negroes and other nonwhite races.
[b] Operatives
Source: U.S. Dept. of Labor, *The Social and Economic Status of Negroes in the United States* (Washington, D.C.: U.S. Government Printing Office, 1969), p. 41.

Table 2-6.  Percentage Distribution of Nonwhite Male Employment
by Industry and Index of Industrial Affiliation, 1964

| Industry | Percent male nonwhite of total male | Index of industrial affiliation of nonwhite males (National nonwhite index = 100) |
|---|---|---|
| Construction | 10.7 | 111.45 |
| Manufacturing | 7.8 | 82.97 |
| Furniture and fixtures | 7.5 | 79.78 |
| Stone-clay-glass products | 9.6 | 100.00 |
| Fabricated metal products | 7.1 | 73.95 |
| Electrical machinery | 4.8 | 50.00 |
| Transportation equipment | 8.8 | 91.66 |
| Miscellaneous manufacturing | 6.2 | 64.58 |
| Food and kindred products | 10.6 | 110.41 |
| Textile mill products | 6.8 | 70.83 |
| Apparel | 8.3 | 86.45 |
| Printing and publishing industry | 4.7 | 48.95 |
| Chemicals and allied products | 7.1 | 73.95 |
| Other nondurable goods | 6.5 | 67.70 |
| Transportation and public utilities | 10.1 | 105.20 |
| Trade | 9.1 | 94.79 |
| Finance, insurance and real estate | 5.8 | 60.41 |
| Business and repair services | 9.4 | 97.91 |
| Personal services | 19.4 | 201.04 |
| Entertainment and recreation | 13.0 | 135.41 |
| Professional services | 10.4 | 108.33 |
| Hospital | 22.9 | 238.54 |
| Public administration | 10.3 | 107.29 |

Source: U.S. Dept. of Labor, *The Negroes in the United States, Their Economic and Social Conditions*. Bulletin No. 1511 (Washington, D.C.: U.S. Government Printing Office, June, 1966).

indicates a relative decline in blue collar production workers since 1920, as shown by the dotted line.

The special problem of black workers is that the change in the occupational structure of labor is shifting in the direction of service-producing industries, including those lower-paying service-producing jobs where unskilled black workers are already concentrated. The extent of this concentration by occupation is shown in Table 2-7, which indicates that the proportion of black nonfarm laborers and service workers is almost three and one-half times the propor-

Figure 2-1.   Industrial Distribution of Civilian Employment, 1920–66

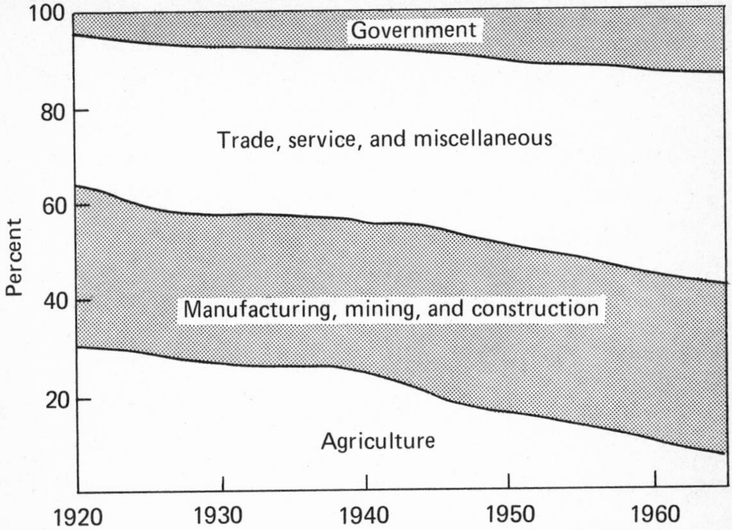

tion of whites, while the proportion of black craftsmen and foremen is only three-fifths the proportion of white in this higher-paying occupation.

The existence of an almost 4 to 1 ratio of nonfarm black laborers to white, as shown in Table 2-7, is occurring at a time when the

Table 2-7.   Occupational Distribution of Year-Round, Full-Time Employed Men, by Color, 1968

|  | Percent distribution | | Index (White = 100) |
|---|---|---|---|
| Occupation | White | Nonwhite |  |
| Total employed | 100.0 | 100.0 | 100.0 |
| Service workers | 5.4 | 17.1 | 316.7 |
| Nonfarm laborers | 3.8 | 14.8 | 389.5 |
| Total | 9.2 | 31.9 | 346.7 |
| Craftsmen and foremen | 21.5 | 12.9 | 60.0 |
| All others | 70.3 | 44.8 | 63.7 |

supply of unskilled black labor is likely to increase rather than diminish. That is, by 1975 nonwhites in the labor force will have increased much faster than whites. This increase will occur between the age of 16 and 24 years, and this nonwhite age group where unemployment rates among blacks are highest will account for more than one-fourth of the total a decade earlier. Thus, by 1975 we may expect a high increase in the proportion of unskilled and inexperienced nonwhite workers, while the most experienced nonwhites (age 25–44 years) will represent a smaller proportion of the labor force in 1975 as compared with 1965.[4]

8. Black workers employed in low-productivity service industries and jobs suffer a loss in real income and employment as the total output of the economy expands. That is, given oligopolistic industries as the center of prosperity in the economy, the expansion of output under conditions of oligopolistic pricing has the following results: (a) Demand is reduced for unskilled labor in manufacturing, particularly ghetto labor, which becomes a special case because black labor is already overrepresented in low-productivity service industries with fixed labor/capital ratios where expansion of output can occur without raising real wages for unskilled labor; (b) White workers, who are already employed in substantially greater proportions than black workers in high-productivity and higher-paying industries, can share the increase in industrial productivity through higher real wages; (c) Black ghetto labor, with fixed wages (the legal minimum), can share in the increased productivity only if industrial prices are reduced in accordance with the increase in industrial productivity, but oligopolistic pricing prevents significant price reduction even under conditions of a recession; (d) The difference in industrial affiliation between white and black labor, accompanied by basic changes in the industrial composition of the labor force (rise in the proportion of the labor force in service employment) together with oligopolistic pricing, reduces the real income of the black ghetto mass of unskilled labor vis-à-vis the real income of white labor; (e) If the economy were perfectly competitive in the final product market, workers who are concentrated in low-productivity and low-paying industries with limited industrial mobility

⁴ U.S. Department of Labor, *Manpower Report of the President* (Washington, D.C.: U.S. Government Printing Office, 1968).

Table 2-8.  Median Gross Weekly and Hourly Earnings
of all Ghetto Workers in Central Cities, 1959–67

| | Current prices | | | 1957–59 prices[a] | | |
|---|---|---|---|---|---|---|
| Year | Actual weekly | Hourly | Legal min.[b] hourly | Actual weekly | Hourly | Legal min.[b] hourly |
| 1959 | 54.31 | 1.38 | 1.25 | 53.50 | 1.34 | 1.23 |
| 1967 | 61.84 | 1.55 | 1.40[c] | 53.17 | 1.33 | 1.20 |

[a] Earnings in current prices divided by the consumer price index.

[b] Workers in private employment subject to a minimum wage under the Fair Labor Standards Act.

[c] For workers already covered, the 1966 amendments raised the specified minimum from the previous $1.25 an hour to $1.40, effective February 1, 1967, and $1.60 on February 1, 1968.

*Source:* Computed from median earnings of Negro workers in central cities, in U.S. Dept. of Commerce, *Trends in Social and Economic Conditions in Metropolitan Areas, Current Population Reports,* Series P-23, No. 27 (Washington, D.C.: U.S. Government Printing Office, 1969), p. 47.

could share in the increase in productivity of high-productivity and higher-paying industries, and increases in productivity would pass to the consumer in the form of lower prices, thereby raising the real income of all workers.

The tendency of real wage rates among ghetto dwellers as a whole to fall or not to rise far above the real wage equivalent of the minimum legal rate is shown empirically in Table 2-8. It is noted that although hourly rates in current prices increased from $1.38 in 1959 to $1.55 in 1967 (an increase of 12.3 percent), real hourly rates fell by 0.6 percent. Also, the legal hourly rates rose in money terms by 12 percent over the period but there was a fall of 2.4 percent in the real wage equivalent of the legal money wage. Thus, there was a fall in both the actual hourly real rates of ghetto dwellers and the hourly real wage equivalent of the legal minimum. The difference between the actual hourly real wage and the hourly real wage equivalent of legal money wage was 11 cents in 1959 and 13 cents in 1967.

The large and growing supply of unskilled black labor in the face of a falling demand in manufacturing will continue to depress the money wage rates of ghetto workers. As employment opportunities for unskilled manual labor in manufacturing shrink, black

Table 2-9.  Index of Change in Productivity in Manufacturing, Real Wages of All Workers in Manufacturing and Black Workers in Central City, with Percentage Change in Real Wages, 1959–67

| | | Real wagesᵇ in 1957–59 prices | | | |
| Year | Outputᵃ per manhour in manufacturing (1957–59 = 100) | All workers in manufacturing (weekly) | Black workers in central city ghettosᶜ (weekly) | Percent change 1959–67 all workers in manufacturing | Black ghetto workers |
|---|---|---|---|---|---|
| 1959 | 103.7 | $86.96 | $53.50 | | |
| 1967 | 133.5 | 98.80 | 53.17 | 113.6 | 99.4 |

ᵃ Establishment basis.

ᵇ Earnings in current prices divided by consumer price index.

ᶜ Includes median earnings of nonfarm laborers and all service workers.

*Source: Economic Report of the President,* February 1968, pp. 247, 248; U.S. Dept. of Commerce, Bureau of the Census, *Current Population Reports,* Series P-23, No. 27 (Washington, D.C.: U.S. Government Printing Office, 1969), pp. 47–48.

workers must seek jobs in lower-paying service-producing jobs and industries (trade and service industries).

In short, black workers are primarily unskilled and are paid to a great extent the legal minimum wage. In a period of prosperity and rising prices, their real income falls because product prices are rising. In the long run, technological change reduces the demand for unskilled labor in high-productivity manufacturing employment and thus black workers are faced with declining economic opportunity. If the economy were perfectly competitive, rising productivity would lead to falling product prices rather than rising wages for the skilled and organized.

This argument implies the following supporting hypotheses:

1. That the real income of black workers in central city ghettos has fallen as a result of the failure of product prices to fall as productivity rises.

2. That real wages of unskilled black workers fall during business expansion.

3. That technological change in manufacturing has reduced the demand for unskilled black workers in manufacturing.

The effects of oligopolistic pricing upon the real income of black ghetto workers in low-productivity employment is shown in Table 2-9.

In terms of price level changes over the eight-year period, 1959–67, the median income of ghetto workers should have risen by 15 percent to maintain the same real income. Instead, ghetto workers' real income fell by 0.6 percent. Productivity in manufacturing, however, rose over the period (1957–59 = 100) from 103.7 in 1959 to 133.5 in 1967, a net rise of 29.8 percent. The real wages of workers in manufacturing rose by 13.6 percent. If the economy were perfectly competitive, the rise in productivity of 30 percent over the period would have led to a fall in product prices instead of a rise in real wage of the skilled and organized by 13.6 percent.

Now, if industrial prices over the period had been cut by, say 24 percent, in terms of the rise in productivity by 30 percent, the real income of all workers could have risen by 30 percent by price reductions. In the case of ghetto earners, a 30 percent rise in real wages by price reductions would have caused an increase in the median real wage of ghetto workers from $2,782 in 1959 to $3,616.60 in 1967 instead of a decrease to $2,765. This meant a real loss of $834.60 in ghetto worker median income between 1959 and 1967, due to the absence of a perfectly competitive economy.

But since the economy is oligopolistic, prices do rise, notwithstanding rises in productivity. Thus the median ghetto worker, between 1959 and 1967, lost $17.00 in real income due to price level changes, and $834.60 in terms of the failure of industrial prices to fall proportionate to the rise in industrial productivity. The total loss was $851.60.

## THE FALL IN DEMAND FOR UNSKILLED LABOR IN MANUFACTURING

Between 1950 and 1960, as previously mentioned, the number of men's laboring jobs in manufacturing fell by 20 percent.[5] Since 1960, the fall in demand in manufacturing industries for the growing supply of unskilled black labor is shown in Table 2-10, which in-

[5] United States Department of Commerce, Bureau of the Census, "Detailed characteristics, U.S. Summary," *U.S. Census of Population, 1960* (Washington, D.C.: U.S. Government Printing Office, 1960).

Table 2-10.  Changes in Manhour Productivity, Proportion of
Manufacturing Employment, Nonfarm Labor Proportion of Total
Employment, and Changes in Employment of Nonfarm Negro
Labor, 1960–75

| | Actual | | | Projected | |
|---|---|---|---|---|---|
| Item | 1960 | 1965 | 1968 | 1970 | 1975 |
| Index of total private output per manhour, labor force basis (1957–59 = 100) | 104.5 | 125.0 | 138.2 | | |
| Percent manufacturing employment of total | 31.0 | 29.7 | | | 25.9 |
| Percent change (1960 = 100) | 100.0 | 95.8 | | | 83.5 |
| Percent nonfarm labor of total employment | 5.5 | 5.3 | | 3.7 | 3.7 |
| Percent change (1960 = 100) | 100.0 | 96.3 | | 67.2 | 67.2 |
| Number of Negroes employed as non-farm laborers | 951,000 | | *875,000 | 868,000 | 860,000 |
| Percent change (1960 = 100) | 100.0 | | 92.0 | 91.3 | 90.4 |

* Figure is for 1969.

Source: U.S. Dept. of Labor, *Economic Report of the President,* January 1969, p. 266; *Manpower Report of the President.* April 1967, p. 274 and April 1968, p. 304; and *The Social and Economic Status of Negroes in the United States,* 1969, p. 41 (Washington, D.C.: U.S. Government Printing Office).

dicates that between 1960 and 1968, productivity (1957–59 = 100) increased 33.7 percent thereby causing a fall in the proportion of total employment in manufacturing. The percent nonfarm labor of total employment (1960 = 100) is projected to drop to 67.2 percent by 1975, while number of Negroes employed as laborers shows a projected drop of roughly 97,000, or 10 percent by 1975.

The fall in demand for unskilled black labor in manufacturing is graphically illustrated in Figure 2-2 where the point $E$ represents the initial equilibrium of supply and demand of unskilled black workers in manufacturing industries at some real wage, $W^m$. The demand for unskilled black labor in manufacturing in this initial period ($t$) as represented by $dt$ $dt$ is $OY$ amount of unskilled black labor at the wage $W^m$. As time goes by we observe two things:

Figure 2-2.    Annual Losses in Aggregate Real Income
of the Black Ghetto

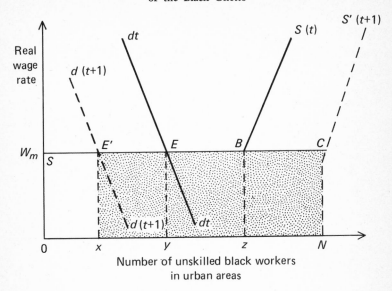

Number of unskilled black workers
in urban areas

(1) the supply curve of black labor remains infinitely elastic at the real wage $W^m$ and increases from $OZ$ in period $(t)$ to $ON$ in period $(t+1)$; and (2) the demand curve in period $(t)$ shifts leftward from $OY$ in period $(t)$ to $OX$ in period $(t+1)$ as manufacturing output expands. So we notice a new equilibrium at point $E'$ of the supply of and demand for black unskilled workers in manufacturing at the real wage $W_m$. Equilibrium employment at this wage has decreased from $OY$ to $OX$ but the number of unskilled black workers seeking production work has increased from $OZ$ to $ON$. Thus, we have $XN$ amount of surplus black labor for higher-paying production work that places a downward pressure upon the real wage income of the black community, which loses annually the amount of real income in manufacturing represented by the rectangle $E'XNCE'$ in Figure 2-2. As time goes by, technological changes in manufacturing lessen the demand for unskilled black labor in production work while there are big increases in supply. Therefore, real wage income does not rise, and the black community loses the aggregate real income of the shaded area $E'XNCE'$.

This drop in demand for unskilled black labor in manufacturing

Table 2-11.  Percent Unemployment of Negro Men,
Women, and Teenagers, Central City Ghettos of Six Large Cities[a]
Combined, July 1968–June 1969

| Black ghetto labor force | Unemployed any time during the year[b] |
|---|---|
| Adult Negro men | 20% |
| Adult Negro women | 17 |
| Negro teenagers | 49 |

[a] Atlanta, Chicago, Detroit, Houston, Los Angeles, and New York City.

[b] Unemployment was not confined strictly to the time period of July 1968–June 1969. Depending on the actual week of interview, "any time during the year" could extend as far back as late 1967.

*Sources:* U.S. Dept. of Labor, Bureau of Labor Statistics, and U.S. Department of Commerce, Bureau of the Census, *Current Population Reports,* Series P-23, No. 29 (Washington, D.C.: U.S. Government Printing Office), p. 93.

is reflected in the inordinate rates of unemployment in the black labor force of central city ghettos. This is shown in Table 2-11. As noted earlier, in six cities combined, at any time during the year July 1968–June 1969, unemployed adult Negro men represented 20 percent of the black ghetto labor force, Negro teenagers represented 49 percent, and adult Negro women represented 17 percent.

We have observed that given a large mass of predominantly unskilled black workers in central city ghettos, heavily unemployed, and heavily concentrated in low-productivity service-producing jobs and industries, prosperity and rising prices reduce their real income because product prices are rising. In the long-run, technological change in manufacturing reduces their economic opportunity because technological change in manufacturing reduces the demand for unskilled labor in high-productivity and high-paying manufacturing employment. Rising productivity would lead to falling product prices, rather than rising wages for the skilled and organized, if the economy were perfectly competitive rather than oligopolistic. Therefore, given black labor as predominantly unskilled, we conclude that a major factor in central city ghetto poverty is the unique way in which economic forces (technological and oligopolistic) restrict the rise in real income of the black ghetto community as a whole. This suggests that the approach to ghetto economic development must be in terms of macroeconomic analysis with attention focused upon the ghetto community as an economic aggregate and representing a unique phenomenon apart from the rest of the economy. That is, from the standpoint of economic analysis, we cannot profitably view the black ghetto community as simply a residential area having a spatial dimension where poverty is viewed in individualistic terms, and where welfare measures and policies concerning poverty are tied to this microeconomic view. Such a view omits not only the unique effects of exogenous forces upon continued ghetto poverty, but fails to consider how forces endogenous to the economic structure of the ghetto economy generate a permanent condition of poverty.

*Chapter 3*

# THE GHETTO MARKET SYSTEM AND ECONOMIC STRUCTURE

## THE GHETTO MARKET SYSTEM

In planning the economic development of the black community, we must begin with a consideration of the present conditions of resource allocation within the ghetto before specifying the conditions under which we may expect development to occur. Therefore, the purposes of this chapter are (1) to present a theoretical view of the ghetto market system of resource allocation and (2) to describe empirically the economic structure encompassed by the ghetto market system.

Our frame of reference is a simplified model of the present flow of ghetto resources. The model presupposes that the economic structure of the ghetto is a result of the allocational processes of the ghetto market mechanism, albeit market forces are constrained by racial factors. That is, in both ghetto consumer and producer markets, economic choices with respect to the mobility and utilization of ghetto resources are limited by economic as well as racial factors. For example, it is assumed that low incomes and Negro population density—in a well-defined spatial area with poor quality housing— are concomitant variables reflecting economic as well as racial factors. Our simple model of the ghetto market system will enable us to observe that the structure of the ghetto is the basic determinant of the ghetto income pattern. We shall, therefore, consider first a simple model of the ghetto system and then proceed to fill in the empirical data on the production pattern of the system, based upon detailed studies of several major ghetto communities.

## A Simplified Model of the Ghetto System

Conceptually and analytically, it is convenient to delineate the ghetto sector of the economy as an underdeveloped geographic region commonly known as the black ghetto of central city. This regional concept enables us to account for the totality of resources within a specified geographic area and to observe and measure the flow of all resources into and out of the specific area, whether black-owned or white-owned, and to describe the production pattern (economic structure) that generates the movement of ghetto resources, including white-owned as well as black-owned business firms. Our model classifies the economic units of the area as:

1. Business firms consisting of *black-owned firms* and *white-owned firms*.
2. *Ghetto households* that are predominantly black. Economic units outside the ghetto that benefit from the ghetto area (outside white business firms and households to which ghetto resources flow) are classified as follows: white households outside the ghetto that supply labor and capital to white-owned ghetto businesses are designated as *households in the rest of the economy;* white business firms outside the ghetto obtaining money receipts from ghetto expenditures are designated as *business firms in the rest of the economy.*

Households within the ghetto and business firms (within and outside the ghetto area) interact in six sets of markets: (1) For consumer goods and services supplied by small black-owned business firms, (2) For consumer goods and services supplied by larger white-owned business firms operating in the ghetto, (3) For consumer goods and services supplied by business firms in the rest of the economy, (4) Resource or factor markets of black-owned business firms in the ghetto, (5) Resource or factor markets of white-owned business firms in the ghetto, and (6) Resource or factor markets of business firms in the rest of the economy. These repre-

Figure 3-1.   Circular Flow of Ghetto Resources

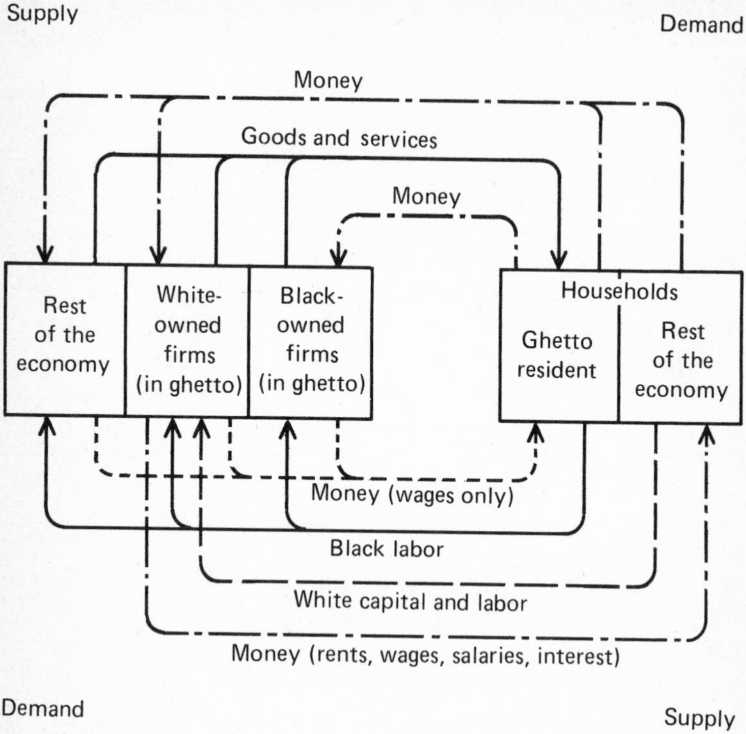

Supply                                                                    Demand

Money

Goods and services

Money

| Rest of the economy | White-owned firms (in ghetto) | Black-owned firms (in ghetto) | Households |  |
|---|---|---|---|---|
|  |  |  | Ghetto resident | Rest of the economy |

Money (wages only)

Black labor

White capital and labor

Money (rents, wages, salaries, interest)

Demand                                                                    Supply

sent the component elements involved in the allocation of resources in the ghetto economy. They form the core around which the economy of the ghetto is built.

The circular flow diagram (Figure 3-1) furnishes the bare elements of the ghetto model of resource allocation. It will be observed that two sets of households supply resources to ghetto business firms and receive payments from these firms. First, the ghetto resident households, which include all individual and family units of the ghetto, furnish mainly labor (managerial, professional, semiskilled, and unskilled) to black-owned business firms whose production activities are primarily services and small retail trade. The factor receipts for the production of these services and retail operations are almost exclusively wages or wages of management. Thus, we get a flow of resources between ghetto households and black-owned business firms, representing supply and demand in the ghetto-owned factors market. This flow, called the *ghetto domestic sector,* consists of small businesses owned and operated by blacks and generating small incomes and residual employment. The ghetto domestic sector will be discussed in detail later.

The second set of households consists of those households in the rest of the economy. These are primarily white households, furnishing white capital and white labor to white-owned business firms operating in the ghetto. It should be noted from Figure 3-1, that in the white-owned ghetto factors market there is some flow of black labor to white-owned business firms operating in the ghetto but the main flow of resources is from the households in the rest of the economy. This flow consists of both capital and labor. Therefore, the return flow of factor payments to ghetto residents is wages only; the return money flow to households in the rest of the economy comprises rents, wages, salaries, interest, and so forth.

It is also observed that the goods and services produced by white-owned firms are purchased only by ghetto residents, while white households in the rest of the economy receiving income from ghetto household expenditures spend their money in the rest of the economy. The flow of factor payments from white-owned businesses in the ghetto goes to households in the rest of the economy, and this part of ghetto-produced income is not returned to the ghetto economy. We observe, therefore, a distinct difference between produced income in the ghetto and received income in the ghetto. This difference between produced income and received income is due to the fact that the bulk of ghetto business receipts go as payments to the owners of the factors of production in the rest of the economy.

Because of this outflow of factor payments to the factors of production in the rest of the economy, we shall designate white-owned businesses operating in the ghetto (chain stores, department stores, wholesale and retail establishments, white-owned apartment buildings, and so forth) as the *ghetto enclave sector.* We now have two observable economic sectors in the ghetto economy; the ghetto domestic sector mentioned above and the ghetto enclave sector. One additional sector represents the overwhelming flow of ghetto black labor to the rest of the economy. This outflow of black labor, designated as the ghetto labor-export sector, represents the principal factors markets for black labor, as well as a principal consumers market from which ghetto households buy. They may buy directly from outside the ghetto area or indirectly through white-owned chain stores located in the ghetto or other ghetto subsidiaries of enterprises in the rest of the economy.

To summarize, the lower half of Figure 3-1 represents supply and demand in the ghetto area factors market. Black labor, the primary ghetto-owned economic resource, flows to the rest of the economy. This labor and white-owned capital, the primary capital resource, together yield returns that flow mainly to white households in the rest of the economy. The upper half of Figure 3-1 shows, on the supply side, consumer supplies from three different markets where the bulk of the market supply comes either from the rest of the economy or from white-owned firms operating in the ghetto. The demand side shows ghetto household expenditures, emanating from money wage payments, only where payments to white-owned capital (rents, interests, and profits) earned in the ghetto together with wages and salaries of white labor earned there become part of the consumer expenditures in the rest of the economy.

We observe, therefore, from our simplified ghetto model, that the flow of money resources in the ghetto is away from what we have designated as ghetto domestic sector. Money resources generated either by factor payments of white-owned ghetto firms or by ghetto household purchases in the form of business receipts of white-owned firms (within or outside the ghetto) continuously flow in the direction of the ghetto enclave sector and the rest of the economy.

Since the circulation of business receipts in the ghetto is away from the ghetto domestic sector, there is no money at the disposal of business firms in this sector for the purchase of ghetto resource services to expand production. The system of ghetto resource organization cannot generate money in the direction of the ghetto domestic sector as long as the enclave sector receives the bulk of aggregate business receipts in the ghetto area. These aggregate receipts represent the total value of produced income in the ghetto and are in excess of the received income of ghetto households. The difference between produced income and received income represents that portion of aggregate business receipts outside the circuit flow of money and goods in the ghetto domestic sector.

In such an environment, the ghetto domestic sector remains an appendage of the more predominant enclave sector, while the ghetto

Table 3-1.  Gross Sales and Race of Owner

| Gross sales | White-owned* | Black-owned* |
|---|---|---|
| $0–2,499 | 4.8% | 21.4% |
| $2,500–4,999 | 4.5 | 14.0 |
| $5,000–7,499 | 4.8 | 12.4 |
| $7,500–9,999 | 4.5 | 7.6 |
| $10,000–19,999 | 8.0 | 14.6 |
| $20,000–49,999 | 20.9 | 16.1 |
| $50,000–99,999 | 21.7 | 8.5 |
| $100,000–199,999 | 13.5 | 3.9 |
| $200,000 and over | 17.3 | 1.5 |
| Totals | 100.0% | 100.0% |

\* Percent of businesses *responding* in each category: 61.0 percent of white-owned businesses; 62.3 percent of black-owned businesses.

*Source: Census of Core Area Businesses*, Eleanor Andreason, Project Director (Buffalo, N.Y.: State University of New York, 1969).

economy as a whole remains static and peripheral to the rest of the economy. This situation exists because the market system and the structure of the ghetto generate an outflow of money and labor resources, leaving a very narrow economic base for the development of the ghetto domestic sector while the ghetto enclave sector receives the bulk of produced income within the ghetto area. An example of the differential in gross business receipts between the black-owned ghetto domestic sector and the white-owned enclave sector is shown in Table 3-1, which indicates gross sales by race of owner in the ghetto of Buffalo, New York.

It will be noted from Table 3-1 that 71.5 percent of black-owned businesses in the Buffalo ghetto had gross sales of less than $20,000, 73.4 percent of white-owned businesses in the Buffalo ghetto had gross sales above $20,000, and almost one-third had gross sales over $100,000. This differential in business receipts between black-owned and white-owned businesses operating in the black ghetto has serious economic and structural implications with respect to the market organization and flow of resources in the ghetto. It implies that, if the income and employment level of the ghetto is to be raised, the economic base of the ghetto domestic sector must be broadened and the structure of the ghetto must be changed.

We shall now turn to a rather detailed empirical analysis of the structure of the ghetto economy, focusing our attention primarily upon differentials between white-owned and black-owned enterprises operating in the ghetto with respect to: (a) form of business organization; (b) levels of investment and trends; (c) types of economic activities; and (d) employment and returns to the factors of production.

## THE STRUCTURE OF THE GHETTO ECONOMY

As shown in Figure 3-1, the direction of the net outflow of money resources from the ghetto is generated by: (a) the black-owned ghetto domestic sector; (b) the white-owned enclave sector; and (c) the black-owned labor export sector. The structure of the ghetto economy may therefore be described as the type, scope, and magnitude of those economic activities that form the pattern of production among these several sectors. This includes the level and trend of investment by type of enterprise and form of production organization. It also includes the effects of such investment upon: (a) employment and business receipts in the ghetto; (b) ghetto factor payments; (c) the extent to which ghetto labor is trained and upgraded; and (d) improvement in wages and working conditions within the ghetto economy.

We shall consider first the structure of the white-owned ghetto enclave sector referred to in our simple model of the ghetto system. Next, we shall discuss the structure of the black-owned ghetto domestic sector also referred to in our model. We shall reserve discussion of the ghetto labor-export sector for later chapters.

### The White-Owned Ghetto Enclave Sector

Our model of the ghetto economy (see Figure 3-1) postulated two markets within the ghetto for the factors of production. In the *factors market of the enclave sector,* the demand side is represented by white-owned business firms operating in the ghetto and the supply side is represented by white households outside the ghetto. In the *factors market of the ghetto domestic sector,* the demand side is represented by black-owned business units and the supply side is represented by black households.

These two markets within the ghetto may be empirically de-

Table 3-2.  Number and Percent of White-Owned Businesses
by Types, Newark Ghetto, August, 1968

|                                          | Number | Percentage |
|------------------------------------------|--------|------------|
| Total retail shopping goods              | 75     | 72.7       |
| General merchandise                      | 6      | 5.8        |
| Apparel group                            | 18     | 17.7       |
| Furniture and household furnishings      | 9      | 8.7        |
| Specialty retail stores                  | 9      | 8.7        |
| Food group                               | 17     | 16.5       |
| Drugs                                    | 3      | 2.9        |
| Building and garden supplies             | 4      | 3.9        |
| Automotive retail                        | 9      | 8.7        |
| Total services                           | 13     | 12.5       |
| Automotive group                         | 5      | 4.8        |
| Building group                           | 2      | 1.9        |
| Miscellaneous services and repairs       | 4      | 3.9        |
| Recreational facilities                  | 2      | 1.9        |
| Total manufacturing                      | 7      | 7.0        |
| Others                                   | 8      | 7.8        |
|                                          | 103    | 100.0      |

*Source:* Governor's Economic Policy Council, "Capital Expansion Possibilities, Newark, N.J., Ghetto, 1968." Unpublished report (Frank G. Davis, Principal Investigator). This report is the source for all Newark data in this volume.

lineated in terms of: (a) the nature and scope of factor demand as shown by the pattern of productive activities; (b) the form of business organization, that is, the proportion of firms in the two respective markets representing sole proprietorships and corporations; (c) average business receipts; (d) average value of capital investment; and (e) average factor returns and payments. The nature of factor demand as shown by the pattern of productive activities in the ghetto enclave sector is mostly a demand for capital, together with some labor, to be used in retail and wholesale distribution of consumer goods and certain specific types of manufacturing (mostly nonconsumer items).

An indication of the specific pattern of distribution of these white-owned economic activities in the enclave sector of the ghetto may be observed from the results of a study by this writer in the ghetto of Newark, New Jersey.[1] Table 3-2 shows that 72.7 percent

[1] Governor's Economic Policy Council, Frank G. Davis, Principal Investigator, "Capital Expansion Possibilities, Newark, N.J., Ghetto, 1968." Unpublished.

Table 3-3.  Three-Year Combined Average of Gross Sales and Profits
of White-Owned Sole Proprietorships, Newark Ghetto, 1965–67

| Item | Apparel stores | General merchandise | Bakeries confectioneries, and drugs | Automotive services |
|---|---|---|---|---|
| Gross sales per establishment | $87,169 | $46,947 | $94,793 | $45,903 |
| Gross profit | 28,139 | 14,452 | 26,156 | 20,259 |
| Net before taxes | 9,980 | 5,572 | 8,365 | 4,795 |

of white-owned enterprises operating in the Newark ghetto are
enterprises distributing goods shopped at retail (generally excluding
eating and drinking enterprises) and 12.5 percent are enterprises providing services (excluding personal services).

Essentially the same pattern of white-owned business types of
enterprises was found in the Buffalo ghetto, where 62.4 percent of
white-owned business units were engaged in retail and wholesale
trade. In terms of the number of white-owned firms in the ghetto,
the sole proprietorship prevails. Out of an area probability sample
of 162 businesses in the Newark ghetto, 103, or 63.6 percent, were
white owned. Of these, 56.6 percent were sole proprietorships.

## White-Owned Sole Proprietorships

*Average Business Receipts.* Among the various types of white-
owned sole proprietorships in the ghetto, the apparel group of stores
show the largest absolute amount of net business receipts before
taxes (see Table 3-3). This apparel group comprises shoe stores,
ladies'-wear shops, men's-wear shops, and general clothing stores.

*Capital Investment.* Since the largest proportion of white-
owned firms in the ghetto is in the apparel group, white capital investment in this group is illustrative of the demand for capital and
labor among white-owned sole proprietorships. Gross and net capital investment are shown in Table 3-4. Over a two-year period
(1966–67), gross capital investment per business unit averaged a
little over $30,000, including $14,306 in capital equipment. Gross
business receipts over the three-year period (1965–67) averaged
$87,169 per business unit. In other words, the yearly sales of apparel
goods was six times the value of capital equipment.

Table 3-4.  Yearly Average Capital Investment per Business Unit
in Unincorporated Apparel Stores, Newark Ghetto, 1965–67

| Item | Yearly averages | | | Average, all years |
|---|---|---|---|---|
| | 1965 | 1966 | 1967 | |
| Equipment | $10,880 | $11,640 | $20,400 | $14,306 |
| Changes in investment | | 9,000 | 19,142 | 14,071 |
| Gross investment | | 20,640 | 39,542 | 30,091 |
| Minus depreciation | 544 | 582 | 1,020 | |
| Net investment | | 20,058 | 38,522 | 29,305 |

New investments in inventories between 1966 and 1967 more
than doubled and sales fell off, but gross profits as a percent of sales
grew, and so did net profits before taxes as a percent of sales.

*Average Factor Returns and Factor Payments.* In terms of
factor returns among white-owned sole proprietorships, gross profits
per business unit in the apparel group averaged 32.2 percent of gross
sales and net profits before taxes averaged 11.7 percent of sales. In
general, among all white-owned shopping groups operating as sole
proprietorships in the ghetto, net profits as a percent of sales (before
taxes) averaged between 9 and 12 percent (see Table 3-5). Total
salaries and wage payments per business unit averaged $10,417, rep-
resenting a labor cost of 11.9 percent of gross sales, and was about
equal to 11.7 percent of gross sales going to net profits. Considering
the fact that the total salary and wage costs per business unit was
only $10,417, however, it is obvious that most, if not all of this
amount, went to the one-man managements. Data from the Buffalo
study indicate that 37.2 percent of white-owned firms operating in
the Buffalo ghetto employ no full-time employees, 52.5 percent employ no part-time employees, and 59.3 percent employ no relatives.

Table 3-5.  Profits as Percent of Gross Sales Among White-Owned
Sole Proprietorships, Newark Ghetto, Three-Year Average, 1965–67

| Shopping group | Gross profit of gross sales | Net profits (before taxes of gross sales) |
|---|---|---|
| Apparel stores | 32.3% | 11.7% |
| Bakeries, confectioneries, and drugs | 27.6 | 8.8 |
| General merchandise | 30.1 | 11.8 |
| Automotive services | 44.1 | 10.4 |

Of those employing relatives, 31.2 percent employ only one relative.

*Conclusions.*  Using the apparel group as illustrative of the demand for resources among white-owned sole proprietorships operating in the black ghetto, we arrive at the following conclusion:

1. A white-owned sole proprietorship in the ghetto, operating in the retail apparel trade, is profitable but has shown little evidence of potential growth. The average investment is around $30,000, which generates business receipts of approximately three times the gross amount invested.

2. Factor returns generated by the investment indicate that for every $100 of sales receipts, approximately $12 go to net profits before taxes and $12 go to wages and salaries. Both profits before taxes, as well as wages and salaries, constitute a wage of management that accrues almost exclusively to the owner-manager. That is, individual white-owned single proprietorships in the ghetto, though profitable as a means of individual employment of the entrepreneur, do not represent a demand for employees within or outside the ghetto.

## White-Owned Corporate Activities

In the Newark ghetto, 32 percent of the white-owned firms in the nonmanufacturing category (wholesale and retail trade and miscellaneous convenience goods and services) were corporations. All of the manufacturing firms were incorporated. These manufacturing firms, representing 7 percent of the enterprises, produced apparel and other finished goods, chemicals and allied products, and fabricated metals.

The Buffalo ghetto study indicates that 33 percent of white-owned firms in the Buffalo ghetto are corporations. Manufacturing enterprises in the Buffalo ghetto represent 11 percent of the total business types. While there was no indication of the extent to which white-owned wholesale and retail enterprises in the Buffalo ghetto were incorporated, these wholesale and retail enterprises comprised 62.4 percent of the total white-owned enterprises; 18.1 percent of the white-owned retail establishments were grocery supermarkets, which were undoubtedly incorporated and operating mostly as chain stores.

It is clear that in the wholesale and retail field, a substantial proportion of the white-owned firms in the ghetto are incorporated,

Table 3-6.  Average Gross Sales and Profits per Business Establishment in Wholesale and Retail Trade Under White Ownership, Newark Ghetto, Classified by Form of Business Organization, 1965–67

|  | White-owned ghetto sole proprietor | White-owned ghetto corporation |
|---|---|---|
| Average gross sales per establishment | $68,703 | $534,505 |
| Average gross profit (percent of sales) | 35.5% | 24.2% |
| Average net profits (percent of sales) before taxes | 10.7% | 4.1%* |

\* Includes compensation of corporate officers.

particularly in the ghetto food market. Although these incorporated food chains are less numerous than the sole proprietorship, the value of gross sales is, of course, much larger. In the Newark ghetto, one food chain store revealed gross sales of $500,000 for each of three years, 1965, 1966, and 1967. We shall now consider corporate business receipts, investments, and factor payments among these white-owned nonmanufacturing corporate activities in the ghetto economy.

*Corporate Business Receipts.*  There is a substantial difference between average gross sales per business unit of white-owned sole proprietorships in the ghetto and white-owned corporations, all operating in the wholesale and retail trade of the ghetto. Table 3-6 shows that among sole proprietorships in the retail and wholesale field, average gross sales per establishment was $68,703; among the white-owned corporate establishments in the wholesale and retail field, the average gross sales per establishment was $534,505, or almost eight times as large. Among the sole proprietorships, average gross profit, as percent of sale, was 35.5 percent; among the corporations it was 24.2 percent. And average net profit as a percent of sale before taxes was 10.7 percent among the sole proprietorships and 4.1 percent among the corporate-owned enterprises.

*Corporate Investments.*  It is noted from the data in Table 3-7 that in the period 1965–67 the yearly average value of corporate equipment per business unit was $100,313 and that there was an average increase in inventory of $158,028. The average annual net investment was $284,425 per establishment. This investment generated annual gross profits of $129,173 per establishment.

Table 3-7.  White-Owned Corporate Retail and Wholesale
Business Investment, Newark Ghetto, 1965–67

| | Capital investment per firm | | | |
| Item | 1965 | 1966 | 1967 | Yearly average |
|---|---|---|---|---|
| Equipment | $34,804 | $127,060 | $139,040 | $100,313 |
| Changes in investment | — | 688,853 | −372,797 | 158,028 |
| Gross investment | — | 815,913 | −233,757 | 291,078 |
| Depreciation | 1,742 | 6,353 | 6,952 | 5,016 |
| Net investment | — | 809,560 | −240,709 | 284,425 |

*Effects of Ghetto Corporate Investment upon Factor Payments.*
The individual ghetto corporation in the wholesale and retail
trade, as shown in Table 3-8, generates an annual total of $79,524
in factor payments (profits and compensation of officers, rents, interest, salaries, and wages). These factor payments are three times
that of the sole proprietorship in the ghetto. For every dollar change
in net investment the ghetto corporation generates 14 cents in wages
and salaries, 8 cents in compensation to corporate officers, 5 cents in
rents, and about 2 cents in interest payments. In general, every dollar of change in net investment in the ghetto corporation generated
about 29 cents in payments to the factors of production.

The white-owned corporate organization in the predominantly
retail and wholesale trade of the ghetto generates on the average a
substantially larger volume of factor payments than sole proprietorships do. Salaries and wage payments per corporate establishment are

Table 3-8.  Average of Factor Payments per Corporate Establishment,
Wholesale and Retail, 1965–67

| | 1965 | 1966 | 1967 | Annual average |
|---|---|---|---|---|
| Compensation of officers | $14,364 | $22,372 | $18,683 | |
| Net profits | 144 | 7,220 | 2,943 | |
| Total returns to managment | 14,408 | 29,392 | 21,626 | 21,788 |
| Rents | 9,676 | 15,576 | 15,507 | 13,586 |
| Interest | 1,572 | 5,745 | 6,523 | 4,613 |
| Salaries and wages | 8,052 | 63,843 | 46,716 | 39,537 |
| Total | | | | $79,524 |

almost four (3.8) times greater, rent payments are almost twelve (11.9) times as large, and compensation to management (payments to corporate officers or wages of management of the sole proprietorship) is almost twice (1.8) as large.

The concentration of the white-owned enclave sector of the ghetto in the ghetto consumer market for shopping goods represents a highly profitable operation. Sole proprietorships in the apparel field indicate that for every dollar change in net investment, $2.97 in sales arises, and for every dollar change in net investment 73 cents are generated in the form of net profits, wages and salaries, and rent. Among the corporations in the retail and wholesale field, for every dollar change in inventory there is 50 cents change in factor payments. These business receipts and factor payments of white-owned individual proprietorships and corporations suggest that many of the white-owned businesses in the ghetto are not merely "mom and pop" operations. The returns per dollar of investment for shopping goods in the wholesale and retail trade is highly competitive with the returns on capital in similar activities in the rest of the economy. The profitability of the ghetto market area is due primarily to the large number of people concentrated within a well-defined area who must buy consumer goods and services, either with pay checks or welfare checks. In this respect, we may view the white enclave sector of the ghetto as a supplier of an area or spatial demand, where geographic and transportation factors as well as the racial factors delineate both the consumer market area and the demand.

*Effects of the Profitability of Enclave Sector upon the Ghetto Domestic Sector.* In our theoretical model of the ghetto economy (Figure 3-1), we showed that the flow of resources in the enclave sector (the demand for factor supplies) short-circuited the ghetto-owned domestic sector (black-owned businesses and black households). Empirical evidence for this is shown in terms of the effect of enclave investment upon: (a) rate of employment (employment per dollar of sales) and the use of black labor; (b) black suppliers as a source of hired services (outside of regular employment) such as accounting, insurance, equipment maintenance; vehicle and property maintenance, building construction, or printing; and (c) black suppliers as a source of produced goods such as inventory purchases, equipment, or fuel.

Table 3-9.  Percentage Distribution of White-Owned Firms
by Number of Full-Time Employees

| Number of full-time employees | White-owned firms |
|---|---|
| None | 37.2% |
| 1 | 14.5 |
| 2 | 10.6 |
| 3 | 6.3 |
| 4 | 6.5 |
| 5–9 | 10.6 |
| 10–14 | 3.7 |
| 15 or more | 8.4 |
| No answer | 2.2 |
| Totals | 100.0% |

Approximate total employees   3,300

Source: Census of Core Area Businesses, Eleanor Andreason, Project Director (Buffalo, N.Y.: State University of New York, 1969).

*Employment and Wage Rates of Black Labor in the Enclave Sector.*  The rate of employment of black labor in the white enclave sector of the ghetto depends primarily upon the nature of the production pattern and the labor requirements generated by the pattern. It appears that ghetto corporate investment in the wholesale and retail field, while profitable, does not generate a high rate of employment per establishment.[2] Empirically, an average annual net investment of $284,425 per establishment with an average annual gross sales of $534,404 per establishment will generate an average annual wage bill of only $39,535. This of course excludes the compensation of officers per establishment of $18,473. Now, if we take the annual average wage and salary per employee, which was $4,166.76, and the annual average wage and salary bill of $39,535 per establishment, we observe that the average number of wage and salaried employees per establishment would be limited to nine. And this number is just about equal to the mean of the frequency distribution of the number of employees per establishment in the Newark ghetto.

[2] The study of Newark ghetto businesses took place in an area comprising 303 blocks, with stores in a population 95 percent black. The block sampling fraction was 9/303 and a 100 percent selection was made of all business in the sample blocks. See methodology at the end of this chapter.

The Buffalo ghetto study also shows a range of 5–15 employees or more among the upper 25 percent of the distribution, which would be applicable to ghetto corporations.

The number of employees and percentage distribution in white-owned firms in the Buffalo ghetto is shown in Table 3-9. From this data together with the Newark data, it is estimated that about 20 to 30 percent of the firms in the ghetto employ beween eight and ten full-time workers; 40 percent hire none; and another 40 percent employ between 2 and 3 full-time workers.

So we may say that because of the nature of the production pattern in the white-owned enclave sector of the ghetto, employment is limited. This would be so even if the enclave sector employed all black labor. Since the owners, officials, managers, and supervisors are generally white, however, black employment is more restricted to lower limits of the wage scale where 52 percent earn less than $90 per week. The average weekly wage of black workers employed in white-owned establishments in the Newark ghetto is $75.46 per week, while the average weekly wage of white workers is $84.80 per week. The differential reflects higher job categories among white employees.

*Black Suppliers as a Source for Goods and Services.*    If ghetto enclave sector activities do not represent a significant demand for the labor of black households in the ghetto, is it likely that these enclave activities create a derived demand for black suppliers of goods and services, such as fuel, equipment, and inventories, or re-

Table 3-10.  **Negro Suppliers of Goods and Services to White-Owned Businesses, Buffalo Ghetto**

| Number of Negro suppliers | White-owned firms |
|---|---|
| None | 66.2% |
| 1 | 6.9 |
| 2 | 4.1 |
| 3 | 2.9 |
| 4 or more | 2.0 |
| No answer or do not know | 17.9 |
| Totals | 100.0% |

Source: *Census of Core Area Businesses*, Eleanor Andreason, Project Director (Buffalo, N.Y.: State University of New York, 1969).

pairs, maintenance, construction, account services, and the like? Generally, the answer is no. The extent of the demand for black suppliers of white-owned ghetto businesses is shown in the Table 3-10. The table shows that two-thirds of white-owned businesses in the ghetto do not purchase producer goods and services from black-owned businesses and households, and only 2 percent have four or more black suppliers. Of course, one could argue that black suppliers do not exist. Our answer is that neither does a white demand exist for more black suppliers.

## Conclusion

The economics of the present ghetto case is that in the ghetto area as a whole there is a tremendous volume of aggregate black consumer demand, but the ownership and flow of capital resources and the pattern of production are not geared to generate a flow of resources to the black-owned domestic sector, as will be shown shortly. Capital flows into the ghetto and flows right out again. There is no completion of the circuit flow of money and goods within the ghetto economy as a whole. Hence, if the inflow and outflow of resources tend to equalize, there is very little likelihood of an aggregate net change in the level of capital investment. Even if there were a net change in the level of net investment in the white-owned enclave sector, this would not provide much in the way of economic benefit to the ghetto-owned domestic sector. So, if the ghetto domestic sector is to grow, it must do so by supplanting the enclave sector. But this cannot be done by competitive market forces within the present structure of the ghetto economy. However, as a result of exogenous forces, that is, the black power force, there is always the possibility that the white-owned businesses may move out. We shall now consider this possibility as seen by the white businessmen now operating in the ghetto.

*Economic Outlook.* The data for this section is taken entirely from the Buffalo ghetto study, which shows the response of white-owned business firms in the ghetto to the following questions concerning an appraisal of their businesses there. Positive answers given by the largest and smallest percentage of the respondents are listed.

How successful have you been?
*Somewhat successful,* 61.2%      *Very successful,* 1.8%

Would you do it again?
> Yes, 57.3%    No, 30.0%

Does business plan to move?
> *Definitely not,* 45.0%    *Definitely will move,* 10.0%

Do you plan to cease operations or sell?
> *Definitely not,* 45.0%    *Definitely will cease,* 80.0%

New products or services to be added?
> *Definitely not,* 46.7%    *Definitely will add,* 4.5%

Addition of major equipment?
> *Definitely not,* 50.7%    *Definitely will add,* 4.6%

Remodeling plans?
> *Definitely not,* 52.8%    *Definitely will remodel,* 6.3%

Additional employees planned?
> *Definitely not,* 42.1%    *Definitely will add,* 4.7%

Over 60 percent of the white-owned businesses in the Buffalo ghetto feel that they have been successful, and 57.3 percent say they would operate the business again; only 10 percent say they definitely will move. In general, it appears that over half the white-owned businesses in the Buffalo ghetto feel they have been successful and will not move.

It appears, however, that about half of the white-owned businesses, presumably those who definitely do not plan to move, say that they definitely will not undertake any new investment. That is, they definitely will not add new products or services, make major additions to equipment, remodel or increase their employment. An average of less than 5 percent say they definitely will undertake new investment.

*Prospects for the Future.* This picture of white-owned businesses in the Buffalo ghetto leads us to the general conclusion that there is a great deal of uncertainty about the future of white-owned businesses in the ghetto. Many of the marginal and unsuccessful firms will probably move or cease operations while the successful ones will remain but will not expand. To the extent that this is the general case, the results will be as follows:

1. The white-owned enclave sector will continue as an economic and competitive obstacle to the expansion of the ghetto-owned domestic sector.

2. Capital investment in the ghetto area economy, by remaining static, will perhaps accelerate the rate of depreciation of the properties and capital stock of the ghetto economy.

3. The already limited impact of new capital investment in the enclave sector upon the ghetto domestic sector will be reduced to zero. That is, the already limited number of new jobs for ghetto residents created by capital expansion in white-owned businesses in the ghetto will no longer exist.

## THE STRUCTURE OF THE GHETTO DOMESTIC SECTOR AND GHETTO ECONOMIC DEVELOPMENT

This grim picture of a cessation of new capital investment in the white-owned enclave sector raises the following questions about the ghetto-owned domestic sector:

1. What are the present structure and prospects of the ghetto-owned domestic sector?

2. If the economic structure of the ghetto is such that economic and market forces (ghetto resource ownership and market structure) prohibit the development of the ghetto-owned sector, what measures (economic and governmental) are required for the economic development of the black ghetto?

We have already defined the ghetto domestic sector as simply a sector of the ghetto economy where there is a flow of resources between black-owned businesses in the ghetto and black ghetto resident households. This flow of resources between black-owned businesses and black households involves both a limited factors market for black households and a limited consumers market for black businesses. We may define the magnitude of the factors market of black businesses as that proportion of aggregate ghetto factor costs incurred by black-owned business in the ghetto economy. We may define the magnitude of the consumer market for black-owned businesses as that proportion of aggregate ghetto consumer expenditures representing business receipts of black-owned businesses.

In this part of our analysis, we shall first show that ghetto purchasing power and aggregate sales or business receipts in the ghetto economy as a whole are quite substantial. Second, we shall show that the economic structure of the black-owned sector is such that its present mode of economic activity and investment will generate only a limited proportion of aggregate ghetto factor costs and returns regardless of the level of aggregate black community income and purchases, thereby having no significant impact upon ghetto employment and incomes. Third, we shall show that as a result of endogenous economic forces within the present ghetto structure this very narrow black-owned economic base cannot expand. If the black-owned domestic sector cannot expand, the ghetto economy as a whole will continue to be afflicted with a demand gap between aggregate ghetto factor costs and aggregate ghetto factor returns (income) to ghetto households. In which case, of course, the gap has to be filled by public welfare expenditures in the ghetto, plus restricted expenditures from earnings of black unskilled labor outside the ghetto economy.

Before giving the specific empirical details of the foregoing objectives, perhaps it will clarify matters to show schematically a working concept of the structure of the black-owned sector in relation to: (a) aggregate ghetto factor costs and returns; (b) aggregate ghetto income and purchases; and (c) the demand gap resulting from the general structure of the ghetto economy.

We can chart these present structural relationships within the ghetto economy by simply showing in a different way our earlier chart (Figure 3-1) of the ghetto model. This we have done in Figure 3-2. It should be noted that the emphasis in Figure 3-2 is upon showing the process of the flow of ghetto factor costs into ghetto incomes and incomes into ghetto expenditures.

We have represented the costs of black capital and labor as constituting a relatively small proportion of aggregate ghetto factor costs, and, accordingly, as a small proportion of black consumer demand as costs become incomes and incomes become black consumer expenditures. It is this limited proportion of aggregate ghetto factor costs, represented by the employment of black capital and labor, and the consequent limited conversion of ghetto factor costs into ghetto incomes and expenditures, that define the limits of the ghetto domestic sector.

We have represented the white households of the enclave sector as receiving the bulk of ghetto factor returns to households where

Figure 3-2.  Flow of Ghetto Factor Costs, Incomes, and Expenditures

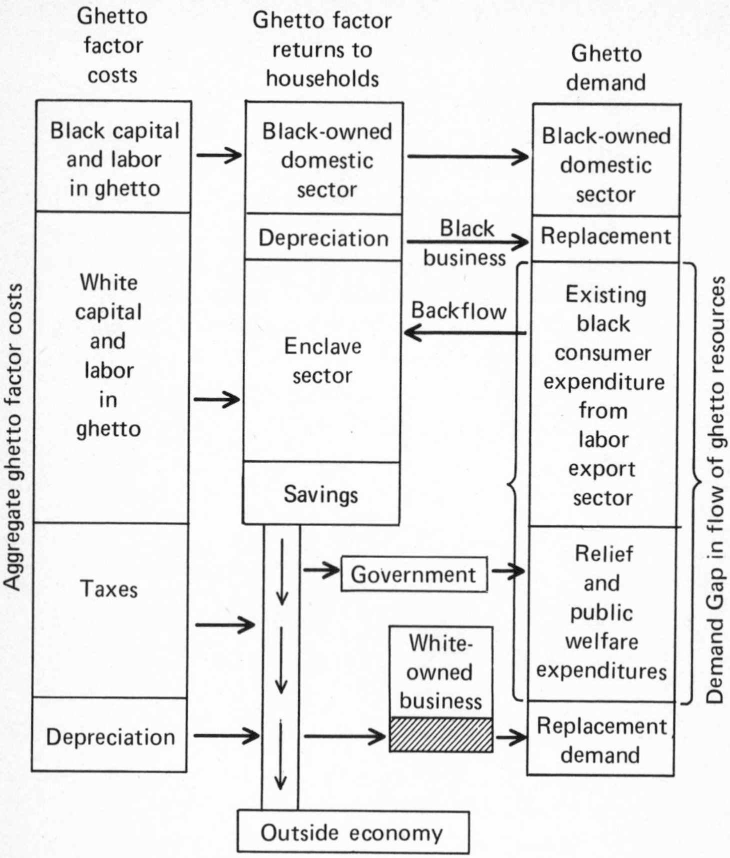

savings occur. The aggregate savings of these white enclave households, however, flow directly to the outside economy rather than to
new capital investments in the ghetto. Hence, we have represented
aggregate gross investment in the white-owned sector as equal only
to aggregate replacement demand. Similarly, we have represented
the black-owned sector as having zero aggregate net investment
largely because there are no aggregate net savings. Thus, there is
only a replacement demand in the ghetto economy insofar as business investment is concerned.

Finally, as a result of the bulk of factor returns and savings going to the enclave sector households that neither purchase goods in the ghetto nor increase aggregate net investments in the ghetto, we have represented this gap in ghetto consumer and business spending as a demand gap. This gap is filled from purchases out of earnings of unskilled black labor employed outside the ghetto plus government (relief and welfare) expenditures.

We shall now proceed in terms of the structural relationship shown in Figure 3-2 to give empirical content to the structure and economic significance of the black-owned domestic sector, and to verify empirically our proposition that, in terms of the present structure of the ghetto market economy as a whole, endogenous or self-sustaining ghetto growth is not feasible and ghetto economic development is impossible under present arrangements. This will continue as long as a substantial demand gap exists between aggregate ghetto factor costs and aggregate ghetto factor returns (income) to ghetto households. We shall elucidate this point shortly. First we shall consider the ghetto market economy as a whole.

## GHETTO PURCHASING POWER

That part of the ghetto economy we have designated as the black-owned ghetto domestic sector is based in an economic area (core area of central city or so-called Model City area) with the following population and economic characteristics:

1. *Population.*  Over 80 percent of the residents of the area are black.

2. *Income of the Area.*  The mean income of black families in the ghetto area is around $5,000.[3] In the Newark ghetto,[4] the mean income in 1966 was roughly $5,542, with the following distribution:

| | |
|---|---|
| Under $3,000 | 23.5 percent |
| $3,000–6,999 | 50.5 percent |
| 7,000–9,999 | 16.9 percent |
| 10,000 and over | 9.2 percent |

[3] In the Cleveland Hough Area, the median income adjusted for price changes in 1964 dollars was $4,772 in 1965.

[4] Computed from Population and Labor Force, Newark, N.J., Research Section, Rutgers University.

Table 3-11.  Negro Family Expenditures and Family Characteristics
by Income Group, 1960–61

|  | Income | | |
|---|---|---|---|
|  | Under $3,000 | $3,000 –7,499 | $7,500 and over |
| Total expenditures | 100 | 100 | 100 |
| Three basic expenditures | 64 | 57 | 53 |
| Food | 29 | 25 | 21 |
| Shelter | 25 | 19 | 16 |
| Clothing | 10 | 13 | 16 |
| All other expenditures | 36 | 43 | 47 |
| Household operations | 11 | 11 | 13 |
| Medical care | 5 | 5 | 4 |
| Transportation | 6 | 13 | 14 |
| Miscellaneous | 14 | 14 | 16 |
| Family characteristics |  |  |  |
| Size (number of persons) | 2.4 | 3.8 | 4.1 |
| Percent who own home | 24 | 33 | 54 |
| Percent who own a car | 17 | 59 | 88 |

Source: U.S. Dept. of Commerce, Bureau of the Census, Current Population Reports, Series P-23. No. 24 (Washington, D.C.: U.S. Government Printing Office, October 1967), p. 61.

3. *Family Expenditures and Characteristics.*  This is shown in Table 3-11.

On the basis of the above characteristics, if we take the Newark ghetto as an example, we can make several observations with respect to ghetto purchasing power. First, we note that the Newark ghetto had a black population of 86,479 in 1966 or 42 percent of the total Newark black population. Now, assuming an average Negro family size of 3.4 persons, there were 25,432 families in the Newark ghetto with an average family income of at least $5,000. This yielded an aggregate purchasing power of more than $127 million[5] in the Newark ghetto in 1966, or a ghetto per capita purchasing power of $1,470.

[5] This figure of $127 million is not of credit purchases plus expenditures out of welfare receipts. Total purchases including credit and transfer payments in the Newark ghetto in 1966 was $215.7 million, indicating an increase of purchases of about 70 percent above cash receipts.

Table 3-12.  Business Ownership, Buffalo Ghetto, by Race of Owner

| Form of ownership | White-owned (percent) | Black-owned (percent) |
|---|---|---|
| Corporation | 33.0 | 5.4 |
| Partnership | 13.0 | 10.8 |
| Single proprietorship | 54.0 | 83.0 |
| Other | | 0.2 |
| No answer or do not know | | 0.6 |
| Total | 100.0 | 100.0 |

Source: Census of Core Area Businesses, Eleanor Andreason, Project Director (Buffalo, N.Y.: State University of New York, 1969).

If we assume that, as in the Newark case, around 42 percent of black population in metropolitan areas are located in the black ghettos,[6] there would be roughly 8 million black people in the urban ghettos of the United States.

With a ghetto per capita purchasing power of $1,470, we have a national aggregate ghetto purchasing power of $11.8 billion or 32.3 percent of total Negro incomes in 1969.

If we distribute this $11.8 billion according to the pattern of ghetto family expenditures, we have the following results:

| | |
|---|---|
| Food | $ 2.9 billion |
| Shelter | 2.2 billion |
| Clothing | 1.5 billion |
| All other | 5.2 billion |
| Total | $11.8 billion |

A basic question at this point is can the present structure of the black-owned sector be expanded to capture an aggregate ghetto purchasing power of approximately $12 billion? If the answer is no, then the next question is how can the black-owned sector of the ghetto be restructed to capitalize upon a $12 billion ghetto market? The answer to these questions will come later.

## Investment and Factor Employment

In terms of types of economic activity, we may say that the black-owned domestic sector consists mostly of sole proprietorships engaged predominantly in: (a) services, primarily personal; and (b)

[6] The percent of nonwhite families in poverty areas of large cities in 1966 was as follows: All large cities, 62 percent; New York City, 62 percent; Chicago, 54 percent; and Los Angeles, 47 percent.

Table 3-13. Percentage Distribution of Negro-Owned Businesses Among Different Cities, by Types

| Types of businesses | Buffalo survey, July 30, 1969 | National Business League (7 cities)* June 24, 1969 | Washington, D.C. survey, 1967 |
|---|---|---|---|
| Contract construction | 0.8 | | 5.8 |
| Manufacturing | 1.5 | | 1.7 |
| Newspaper publication | | | 1.4 |
| Transportation | 1.0 | | 4.0 |
| Finance and insurance | | | 4.1 |
| Real estate | | | 3.5 |
| Wholesaling | 1.5 | | 1.0 |
| Total services | 48.2 | 41.5 | 44.0 |
| Barber shops and beauty shops | 26.3 | 31.0 | 26.9 |
| Auto and other repair | 6.7 | | |
| Other services | 11.7 | | |
| Dry cleaners | 3.5 | 11.5 | 7.1 |
| Total retail | 46.8 | 57.5 | 34.5 |
| Carry-out shops, delicatessens, grocery stores, and restaurants | 26.4 | 45.5 | 11.6 |
| All other retail | 20.4 | | |
| Service stations | | 12.0 | |
| Unclassified | 0.2 | | |
| Totals | 100.0 | 100.0 | 100.0 |

* The seven cities in the NBL survey were Atlanta, Cleveland, Durham (N.C.), Jackson (Miss.), Los Angeles, Norfolk, and Richmond.

retailing, primarily eating places and food stores. Table 3-12 shows the form of ownership and race in the Buffalo ghetto, July 1969.

It is observed that while sole proprietorships are more numerous in the ghetto economy as a whole, 38 percent of Negro-owned business units are sole proprietorships and only 5.4 percent are corporations. By comparison, 33 percent of the white-owned ghetto firms are corporations.

Various central city surveys as shown in Table 3-13 reveal the following pattern of distribution by types of Negro-owned businesses.

In Table 3-13, we can observe that although there are variations in the percentages among the different surveys, it is clear that black

Table 3-14.   Reasons for Going into Own Business

| | |
|---|---|
| Inheritance | 2.1% |
| "To better myself" | 16.3 |
| Independence | 16.1 |
| Not take orders | 7.5 |
| Escape job insecurities | 4.6 |
| Inability to get job | 1.9 |
| Worked for previous owners | 1.9 |
| Experience in this type of business | 7.7 |
| Acquaintance with previous owners | 1.3 |
| Social and family reasons | 7.1 |
| Increase prestige | 2.3 |
| Profit | 10.6 |
| Other | 1.7 |
| No answer or do not know | 2.9 |
| Does not apply | 16.0 |
| Total | 100.0% |

Source: Census of Core Area Businesses, Eleanor Andreason, Project Director (Buffalo, N.Y.: State University of New York, 1969).

business firms are concentrated in two areas: service activities (41 to 48 percent), which are mostly personal services (26 to 31 percent), and retail activities (34 to 57 percent), which are mostly carry-out shops, delicatessens, grocery stores, and restaurants (11 to 45 percent). Contract construction (except in Washington, D.C.), manufacturing, and wholesaling are economically important activities that are noticeably negligible in the black-owned domestic sector. How can we account for the large proportion of businesses in service trades and small retail operations as noted above? Before we answer this question, it is interesting to note what the black entrepreneur gives as his reason for going into business. The reasons as shown by the Buffalo survey are given in Table 3-14.

Table 3-14 indicates that 32.4 percent went into their own business either "to better" themselves or to gain independence; 7.5 percent went in to avoid taking orders. Only 10.6 percent were motivated by profit. Certainly, the economic nature of the service trades makes it possible for someone with little capital to improve his condition by creating a better job for himself, especially considering alternative job opportunities. That is to say, given limited savings, limited access to capital markets, and limited alternative job opportunities, it would be sensible for a ghetto entrepreneur to select a type of entrepreneurial activity that required: (1) a minimum of money and physical capital; and (2) a small investment in human capital (such as a short course in learning to be a barber or beautician). By doing so, he would maximize the wage portion of factor costs in the form of self-compensation for labor services as well as of management, sometimes viewed as profits.

Therefore, we must view the returns from the prevailing mode of black entrepreneurial activity in the black-owned sector as a form of individual wage income or wage supplement in a labor intensive ghetto economy. Viewed in this light, the factors market of the ghetto domestic sector cannot be expected to generate the hiring of new employees, for this sector's market is basically a limited labor market for self-employment. We must therefore assess the economics of this self-employing labor market in terms of the wage returns per dollar of investment by the self-employed; with some allowance, of course, for the psychic income due to the desire to be independent and not take orders from a superior.

In Table 3-15 we computed from our Newark survey the average investment in equipment per firm over a three-year period, together with a three-year average of wages and salaries per firm and the investment/wage ratio. The table shows that the average yearly wage per establishment in the black-owned sector ranged from $3,344 in personal service trades to $3,633 among eating and drinking establishments. This type of wage return obviously constitutes a meager demand for employees. In contrast to the black-owned sector we note that in the white-owned sector of the ghetto, the av-

Table 3-15.  Three-Year Average of Equipment Investment per Firm and Average Wage Bill, Newark Ghetto, 1965–67

| | Black-owned sector | | White-owned sector |
|---|---|---|---|
| Item | Personal services | Restaurants, lunchstands, and taverns | Wholesale and retail corporations |
| Average investment in equipment | $15,840 | $18,220 | $102,820 |
| Average salaries and wages | 3,344 | 3,633 | 40,748 |
| Investment/wage | 4.7/1 | 5/1 | 2.5/1 |

erage wage per wholesale and retail corporate establishment was $40,748; an amount per establishment that does constitute a somewhat significant demand for labor.

If we compare the investment/wage ratio between the black-owned sector and the corporate establishments of the white-owned sector, we observe that in the black-owned sector it takes about $5.00 of investment to generate $1.00 in wages; in the white-owned corporate sector, it takes only $2.50 in equipment to generate $1.00 in wages. The wage income per dollar of investment in the white-owned corporate sector of the ghetto is about twice that of the black-owned sector.

With these economic conditions prevailing, it would pay the black-owned sector as a group to buy out the corporate portion of white-owned sector by transferring their assets to this sector and going to work as employees of this sector. For every dollar of investment transferred to corporate activity in the ghetto, the yield in wage income per dollar of investment would be 2.5/1 instead of about 5/1.

## ECONOMIC POTENTIAL OF THE BLACK-OWNED SECTOR

We shall now return to our earlier question of the economic potential of the black-owned sector with respect to aggregate ghetto purchasing power. First, we will consider aggregate ghetto purchases and the present structural limitations upon black sector sales, in the light of the present internal structural weakness of the black-owned sector. Second, we shall consider present structural limitations upon black sector expansion. In this consideration, our frame of reference will be the present structure of the ghetto economy as a whole.

### Structural Limitations upon Sales

In this section we shall consider the structure of the black-owned sector in terms of its capacity to capture aggregate ghetto purchasing power. Our data indicate that the black-owned sector is not structured to do a large volume of business. This is because the type of enterprises, the form of economic organization, and the productivity of the investment in this sector can generate only a small

Table 3-16.  Yearly Average of Aggregate Ghetto Sales Receipts,
by Factor Payments and Other Costs, Newark Ghetto, 1965–67

|  | Amount | Percent |
|---|---|---|
| Gross sales | $215,749,915 | 100.0 |
| Depreciation | 3,055,140 | 1.3 |
| Factor payments to enclave sector | 55,828,000 | 25.6 |
| Factor payments to black sector | 3,867,500 | 1.8 |
| Other costs and expenses | 153,999,275 | 71.3 |

proportion of aggregate produced income in the ghetto. This means that there will be limited factor employment in the black sector, which leads to limited sales capacity, which, of course, leads to a limited proportion of aggregate ghetto purchases. This result is shown in Table 3-16 and Figure 3-3.

Table 3-16 shows the proportion of the ghetto-produced income out of aggregate purchases going to the black-owned sector. Only 1.8 percent of $215.7 million in gross sales in the Newark ghetto

Figure 3-3.  Relationship of Yearly Average of Aggregate Sales,
Business Payments, and Factor Returns, Newark Ghetto, 1965–67

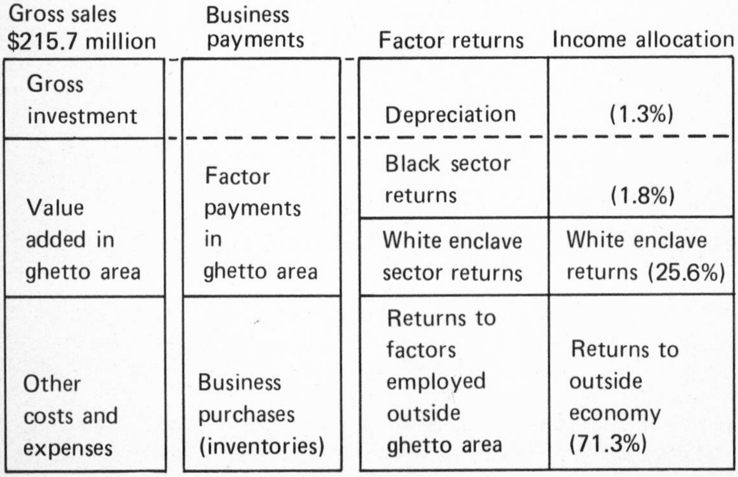

| Gross sales $215.7 million | Business payments | Factor returns | Income allocation |
|---|---|---|---|
| Gross investment | | Depreciation | (1.3%) |
| Value added in ghetto area | Factor payments in ghetto area | Black sector returns | (1.8%) |
| | | White enclave sector returns | White enclave returns (25.6%) |
| Other costs and expenses | Business purchases (inventories) | Returns to factors employed outside ghetto area | Returns to outside economy (71.3%) |

studied goes to the black-owned sector, while 25.6 percent goes to the white-owned enclave sector, and 71.3 percent represents returns to productive factors employed outside the ghetto economy.

Figure 3-3 shows the same results in terms of the operations involved in going from the concept of gross sales to income allocation among the several sectors, indicating that in the ghetto economy as a whole, the present black-owned sector has only marginal capabilities with respect to capitalizing upon the aggregate flow of ghetto resources. Its marginality is inherent in both the forms of its business organization[7] and the type of its economic activity. In terms of form of business organization, we have already noted that the factors market of the black-owned sector is organized almost exclusively as sole proprietorships. Sole proprietorships in general, however, appear to be uneconomic forms of business units and are on the decline[8] in the economy as a whole. Furthermore, we have already shown that wage income per dollar of capital investment in black-owned sole proprietorships constitute less than optimal returns in wages compared with retail and wholesale corporations in the ghetto. Therefore, when we aggregate the capital inputs in black-owned sole proprietorships, we observe a high degree of aggregate capital intensity relative to the results in terms of ghetto incomes. Also, with respect to types of economic activity in the black-owned sector, we note a limited demand for labor, as shown in Table 3-17.

For the type of economic activities characteristic of the black-owned sector, not more than two or three employees are needed and for these types of economic activities, in general, an average of only four employees are used.

We may therefore conclude that the black-owned sector of the ghetto economy is not structured to do a large volume of business or to begin to capture aggregate ghetto purchasing power. Because of the nature of its structure (the miniscule and uneconomic nature of its production pattern) the black-owned sector is marginal with respect to the flow of aggregate ghetto factor costs, incomes, and expenditures in the ghetto economy. Even among sole proprietorships,

[7] In 1964, 23.1 percent of sole proprietorship showed no profit. In 75 percent of profitable business, there was a net profit, and 50 percent showed net profit of less than $2,000. See Internal Revenue Service, *Statistics of Income 1964: U.S. Business Tax Returns*, pp. 19–20.

[8] U.S. Department of Labor, BLS Report 102, *The Negro Job Situation: Has It Improved?* (Washington, D.C.: U.S. Government Printing Office, 1969).

Table 3-17.  Employees per Establishment in Black-
Owned Firms in 1968, and all Firms in 1963,
by Type of Business

| | Employees per establishment | |
|---|---|---|
| Type of business | Black-owned | All firms |
| Laundries | 4.8 | 6.7 |
| Beauty and barber shops | 2.5 | 1.1 |
| Gasoline service stations | 2.3 | 2.5 |
| Food stores | 3.1 | 4.0 |
| Eating places | 1.8 | 6.7 |
| All service and retail | 3.3 | 4.2 |

Source: Project Outreach of the National Business League,
and Bureau of the Census, Census, 1963, Volumes 1 and 7.
From Andrew F. Brimmer and Henry S. Terrell, "The Economic Potential of Black Capitalism," a paper presented at the
82nd Annual Meeting of the American Economic Association,
1969.

which are highly concentrated in the black-owned sector, black-
owned establishments contribute proportionately less to total factor
inputs (factor costs) than various types of white-owned business do,
as shown in Table 3-18.

If we view factor costs as factor payments to households, with
profits as a residual payment, we note from Table 3-18 that factor inputs per establishment in personal services generate only a 9 percent
share of total factor payments per firm, and that factor inputs in
restaurants, lunchstands, and taverns combined constitute about 15
percent of sole proprietorship factor payments. Thus, as shown in
Table 3-18, households in the black-owned sector occupy the following position in order of magnitude with respect to aggregate returns to households from ghetto sole proprietorships:

| | |
|---|---|
| 1. Bakeries, confectioneries, and drugs | 25.9% |
| 2. Apparel stores | 23.0 |
| 3. Automotive services and supplies | 16.7 |
| 4. (Black-owned) restaurants, lunchstands, and taverns | 15.2 |
| 5. General merchandise | 10.2 |
| 6. (Black-owned) personal services | 9.0 |
| Total | 100.0% |

Table 3-18  Average Factor Costs per Establishment Among Sole Proprietorships,
by Type of Business, Newark Ghetto, 1968

| Item of factor costs | Total (sum of averages) | Personal services | Restaurants, lunchstands, and taverns | Bakeries, confectioneries, and drugstores | Apparel stores | Auto services and supplies | General merchandise |
|---|---|---|---|---|---|---|---|
| Total | $100,924 | $9,089 | $15,362 | $26,191 | $23,125 | $16,873 | $10,281 |
| Percent | 100.0 | 9.0 | 15.2 | 25.9 | 23.0 | 16.7 | 10.2 |
| Cost of labor | 14,841 | 974 | 3,214 | 7,803 | 0 | 2,850 | 0 |
| Depreciation | 4,891 | 792 | 911 | 1,046 | 709 | 847 | 586 |
| Taxes on business | 3,969 | 166 | 1,020 | 803 | 1,044 | 594 | 342 |
| Rent | 9,206 | 1,168 | 1,356 | 2,238 | 1,186 | 1,330 | 1,928 |
| Salaries and wages | 31,350 | 3,344 | 3,633 | 6,043 | 10,133 | 6,368 | 1,829 |
| Interest | 533 | 50 | 10 | 286 | 73 | 90 | 24 |
| Net profit | 36,131 | 2,595 | 5,218 | 7,972 | 9,980 | 4,794 | 5,572 |

Our data indicate that even within the ghetto economy the type of sole proprietorship activity that is predominantly black owned generates less in the way of factor payments than many other types of sole proprietorship businesses in the ghetto. Personal service activities, which represent 40 to 50 percent of black-owned businesses, occupy a marginal position in terms of household factor payments.

If we add factor payments of personal services to that of restaurants, lunchstands, and taverns, we note that the factor payments to black households from these predominantly black activities will amount to 24.2 percent of total sole proprietorship payments. However, black households will not receive all of this, since 10 percent of the amount of factor payments that would normally go to black households represents rent on business property that black households do not receive. This reduces the proportion of total sole proprietorship returns going to black households from 24.1 percent to 21.7 percent. The rest of factor payments (78.3) generated by sole proprietorships in the ghetto go to households outside the ghetto area.

Thus we conclude that for the black community as a whole the factors market of black-owned sole proprietorships is only of marginal significance to ghetto households. This would be true even if the black-owned sector of sole proprietorship could be extended to include all presently white-owned sole proprietorships. For, as shown in Table 3-19, household returns from all ghetto sole proprietorships consist of a little more than a third of aggregate ghetto factor payments. Therefore, a further proliferation of black proprietorships under the present structure of the ghetto economy would represent a seriously limited way of expanding the black sector's share of aggregate ghetto business receipts and converting these receipts to

Table 3-19. Three-Year Sum of Average Factor Costs per Establishment, by Type of Enterprises, Newark Ghetto, 1965–67

|  | Amount | Percent |
|---|---|---|
| Total (Three-year sum of averages) | $289,379 | 100.0 |
| Ghetto corporate enterprises | 188,458 | 65.1 |
| Retail and wholesale | 92,388 | 31.9 |
| Miscellaneous convenience goods and services | 96,070 | 33.2 |
| Sole proprietorships | 100,921 | 34.9 |

ghetto household payments. Corporate enterprises in the ghetto capture about two-thirds of ghetto-produced income, imposing serious restrictions upon the economic potential of the black-owned sector as presently structured.

## NOTE ON METHODOLOGY OF NEWARK SURVEY

The survey on which the Newark data are based represents an area probability sample of blocks with stores, drawn with a known probability of 9/303 within the core area (25 central Newark 1960 census tracts) including the target area for the Model Cities proposal. Also, census tracts 40, 50, and 56 were included because of the large number of stores in these tracts.

### Block Listing

All blocks containing stores in the delineated area were listed, a simple random sample of nine blocks was drawn, and all the stores on the sample blocks were completely enumerated. Therefore, the probability of any store being included, the same for all stores, was .0297 even though the number of stores in each block was different.

### Obtaining Estimates

Estimates of sales were computed by summing the total sales or other data of the stores in the blocks included in the sample and multiplying the sample total by the inverse of the sampling fraction; in this case, $1/f$ equals 303/9 or 33.7. After the sample was drawn, the data for the sample list of businesses were abstracted from tax returns by the Internal Revenue Service under its confidentiality requirements. Summary data were provided by IRS without disclosure to the sponsor of any association between tax return information and individual business.

# Chapter 4

# THE EFFECTS OF FACTORS ENDOGENOUS TO THE GHETTO MARKET SYSTEM

## EFFECTS OF THE ENCLAVE STRUCTURE UPON RESOURCE ALLOCATION

In terms of economic structure, the black community takes the form of an enclave of "foreign" or outside producers who own almost all of the private capital resources located in the ghetto area. These privately owned capital resources in the ghetto are employed primarily at the retail and wholesale stages of production. Little or no manufacturing is carried on in the ghetto.

On the supply side, the effect of this enclave structure upon ghetto resource allocation is to confine production and capital spending to the sale of consumer goods—the wholesale and retail distribution of which has very little impact on ghetto employment and income. On the demand side, consumer spending has very little allocational and efficiency effects within the ghetto, since outside factors produce the consumer goods imported to the ghetto.

Whatever allocational or efficiency effects ghetto consumer spending may have outside the ghetto economy, these effects tend to have little or no bearing on capital inflow. This is because profits can be made in the ghetto by the sale of consumer goods there without the movement of manufacturing capital there to take advantage of low-priced labor. In other words, in terms of allocation of resources, particularly labor, the enclave structure of the black community generates employment of labor and capital outside the black community. Meanwhile, black labor in the ghetto community goes unemployed. White capital is not attracted to the community to make use of unemployed labor resources.

The enclave structure of the black community also generates poverty, not only because capital is not attracted, but also because there is an uneconomic combination of labor and capital resources within both the black-owned and white-owned sectors. The combination consist of a motley assortment of small business enterprises with a fixed labor/capital ratio (the owner and a few employees) mixed in with a concentrated residential population. The concentrated residential population generates high economic rent and the small businesses generates a high economic cost of doing business of which the high economic rent is naturally a part. This type of residential-commercial operation raises the cost of living without raising the opportunity of making a living as population expands. It is no wonder that the results are capital deterioration (negative investment) and high unemployment.

## ECONOMIC DISTINCTIONS BETWEEN BLACK AND WHITE COMMUNITIES

If we define the economic structure of the black ghetto as a high-cost residential-commercial operation, we can make an economic distinction between the black ghetto community and nonghetto white communities in which residential and commercial operations are spatially or economically separated. Zoning laws, which provide for this separation, are based upon the principle of efficiency in land use. High-cost commercial land is efficiently combined with high-productivity capital instead of with low-productivity capital in the form of uneconomic business units or deteriorating dwelling units. To combine an efficient factor of production with an inefficient one raises the opportunity cost to the producer and the social cost to the community. Since the existing form of residential-commercial operations of the ghetto represents an inefficient combination of land and capital (the combination of uneconomic business units

Figure 4-1.   Percent of Black Population in Urban Population Density in 1960 and Metropolitan Areas, 1965

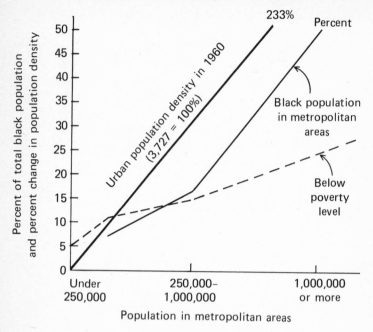

Population in metropolitan areas

Source: BLS Report No. 332; Current Population Reports, Series P-23, No. 24; Bureau of the Census, 1960 Population, Vol. I, p. XIII.

and poor housing units with high-cost land), we may say that the ghetto community has a higher economic and social cost than non-ghetto communities do.

## Effects of the Land/Population Ratio and Land Values

The absence of economic and social mobility for black ghetto residents makes the ghetto community a unique case of high economic and social cost relative to the rest of the economy. This is obvious in the very nature of the economic and demographic structure of the black community. As a result of technological forces in agriculture in the South, where Negroes have formerly lived, the trend has been toward increasing concentration of Negroes in more or less all black areas situated in the heart of the largest metropolitan area.

The trend of this population concentration toward the highest-density urban areas, as shown in Figure 4-1, has increased the ratio of the population to land in central cities along with the rise of the proportion below the poverty level.[1]

In other words, movement of the black migrants to the most densely populated areas, under conditions of housing and economic discrimination has (a) created a problem of land scarcity in urban ghettos and (b) raised ghetto land values[2] relative to the productivity of the labor and capital employed there. That is, the population pressure would cause the land values to rise disproportionately to the rise (if any) in the productivity of the unskilled labor and obsolete capital with which the land is combined.

## Effects of the Land/Population Ratio upon Housing Costs

The rise in land values is caused by the relatively high rent for slum dwelling units whose rents remain high while the quality of the housing deteriorates. Thus, the effects of the rise in ghetto population pressure on a restricted land area is to raise the economic rent. This increase, of course, is reflected in the high institutional rents that reflect higher land values. That is, the high rents represent site values, not the value of the dilapidated buildings and tenements for which ghetto residents pay dearly. We have, therefore, the phenomenon of poor people and poor business resources being combined with high-cost land, where the cost of living on the land (economic rent) gives a larger share of ghetto output to the landlord. That is, the decrease in the land/population ratio causes economic rent to rise relative to the returns to labor and capital. If economic rent rises, institutional rents also rise, even with rent ceilings. The rise in institutional rents occurs when the landlord neglects the cost of maintenance and upkeep and continues to

---

[1] In 1960, the population density in three central cities in the northern New Jersey and New York urbanized area was 24,537. In general, the density of central cities was more than double that of the urban fringe areas—7,788 against 3,200.

[2] Average annual increases in land prices are estimated between 5.0 to 6.0 percent during 1956–66. Residential multifamily land increases most rapidly. Grace Milgram, U.S. *Land Prices—Directions and Dynamics* (Washington, D.C.: U.S. Government Printing Office, 1969), p. 38.

receive a constant or fixed rental rate. Consumers would be paying the same price (rent) for less and less housing services. Thus, the poor are paying more for housing and in the case of the black ghetto the poor are locked into this situation by both economic and racial factors. These factors are involved in the sense that the poor and black are forced to live in the black ghetto where housing costs more. When more is paid for housing in the ghetto, both the quantity and quality of housing remain restricted, resulting in a further rise in housing costs and economic rent as the black population expands.

## The Combination of Low-Productivity Labor and High-Cost Land

If we view the site value of ghetto land in terms of its relatively high economic rent, we must at the same time view the actual and potential productivity of labor on this land. The most abundant productive factor of the ghetto is black labor, which is combined both as laborer and resident with high cost land. In terms of the present industry mix of the ghetto, consisting primarily of small business operations requiring a small and fixed amount of labor per business unit, the growth of the ghetto population reduces the marginal value productivity of labor employed in the ghetto. As time goes on, wage rates in the ghetto will remain low while ghetto employers will find it unprofitable to put ghetto labor to work even at low wage rates. This indicates that a black power system must change the ghetto technology with respect to size and type of ghetto enterprise.

## Effects of High Land Cost per Unit of Capital upon Industrial Location

The rise in ghetto economic rent due to population pressure means that the price of land per unit of capital in the ghetto rises relative to the land cost per unit of capital in less densely populated metropolitan areas. That is, for the individual entereprenuer, the rise in economic rent reduces the marginal value productivity of land relative to its price; and the $\dfrac{\text{marginal value productivity of land}}{\text{price of land}}$ is less

Figure 4-2.  Relative Factor Share by Area: Downtown, Ghetto, and Suburbia

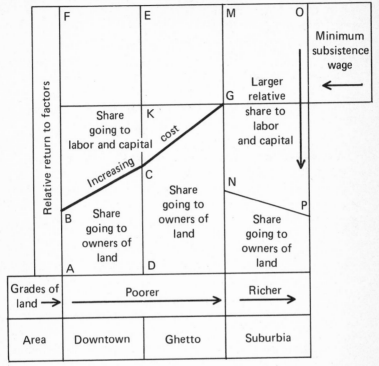

in the ghetto than in the outlying suburbs. The effects of differentials in returns to labor and capital due to differences in the land cost per unit of capital in downtown ghetto and suburban areas are shown in Figure 4-2.

Increasing the ratio of population (labor) to land in the ghetto has caused the marginal value productivity of land to fall per dollar of capital. When this happens, the land cost per unit of capital rises. Assuming no change in technology, a larger share of the community's product goes to the landlord and a smaller share goes to labor and capital. This is shown in Figure 4-2. The area *DCGN* shows that when recourse is taken by the ghetto population (labor) to higher cost land per unit of capital (defined as poorer grade land), diminishing returns occur to both labor and capital. Therefore, the ghetto area under existing technology becomes a high-cost subsistence area. Returns to labor and capital fall from *EC* in downtown to as low as *MG* in the ghetto. At this level, if labor is to be paid its subsistence wage, the return to capital shrinks to zero in the ghetto.

Under the circumstances, assuming no change in ghetto technology, the capitalist seeks a larger return per unit of capital by moving to suburban areas where the land cost per unit of capital is cheaper. This is shown by area *MNPO,* where a larger relative share of the output goes to labor and capital compared with the smaller share of the product that goes to the landlord. The same basic force also operates for the relocation of existing industry outside central cities, as well as the location of new industry outside central cities. As can be seen from the diagram, return on the marginal unit of land of *EC* in the downtown area leaves a margin of *KC* in excess of subsistence wage in contrast to a zero surplus over subsistence in the ghetto. Thus, the black ghetto is left with declining or negative capital investment, increasing cost of production, decreasing return to labor and capital, and a growing supply of unemployed and underemployed black labor due to a shift of industries both from the ghetto and the central cities.

## Effects of Industrial Relocation upon the Supply Cost of Ghetto Labor

Thus, the trend is toward the preemption of industry from an area of relatively high-cost land per unit of capital inhabited by a large available supply of labor. Industrial entrepreneurs are taking recourse to "richer" land (less expensive land per unit of capital in outlying areas). This raises their labor costs vis-à-vis the black labor market in terms of worker transportation cost. That is, lack of established public transportation routes from the ghetto to outlying suburban areas raises the transportation cost of black labor. This higher transportation cost may make the prevailing wage for unskilled labor uneconomic for ghetto labor. The inclusion of the higher transportation cost in the wage would raise the aggregate wage bill for employers and thereby reduce profits. The result is the simultaneous existence of job vacancies and unemployed black labor.

# THE FUNCTIONING OF THE BLACK COMMUNITY AS A SEPARATE ECONOMY

If we define an economy as consisting of the economic processes of production, consumption, and distribution within some specified area, we can say that a subeconomy may develop within a given area of a larger economy to the extent that economic processes in the larger economy generate significant economic and social differentials that represent the factoral conditions of economic separateness. That is, significant area differentials may occur in the production function, the industry mix, the consumption function, and the entire pattern of consumption, where all differentials in these economic processes are occurring within a well-defined spatial area. Wherever these spatial differentials in economic processes exist, there will inevitably follow differentials in economic and social cost between the spatially defined subeconomy and the rest of the economy. These economic and social cost differences may be taken as a criterion of the separateness between the general U.S. economy and the subeconomy of the black ghetto.

## Myrdal's Backwash Effect

The rise of cost differences between the black and white communities throughout the United States are illustrative of Gunnar Myrdal's "backwash effect." In this case, the growing capital-intensive white community has exerted a "strong, agglomerative pull, accelerating their rate of growth, and bringing increasing stagnation" to the labor intensive ghetto economy.[3] We must repeat that this condition of economic stagnation and decay in the black ghettos of America is not self-correcting within the price system. Rather, the pull of economic forces sets up a permanent condition of inequality between a low-income labor-intensive black economy and the rest of the economy. For example, incomes may rise in the white community as national output expands, while at the same time the black community may become relatively poorer. Also, there are differentials in

[3] Gunnar Myrdal, *Economic Theory and Under-Developed Regions* (London, 1957), pp. 13, 28, 29.

the rates of unemployment between the black community and the rest of the economy for any given level of national output.

## Differences in Capital Movements and Resource Allocation

Wage rates and the productivity of capital are lower in the black community, yet capital does not flow to the more labor-intensive black community. The effect of technology is to raise wage rates in the capital-intensive sector while putting downward pressure on wage rates among workers in the already poorly paid labor-intensive black sector. In short, the movement of capital and the allocation of resources in the price system vis-à-vis the black community and the rest of the economy constitute a difference in the kind of capital employed, the kind of production organization, the kind of employment, the kind of income received in the community, the kind of prices paid for goods and services, and the kind of consumption and the nature of consumer demand.

We have already indicated that invested capital in the black community is at the retail stage of production of goods and services, and is characterized by high cost, rising prices and easy credit, high rents, residual employment, and low wages. Therefore, we may say that the black community functions as a separate economy because of the way in which the price system allocates resources to a low-income labor-intensive economy afflicted with a permanent condition of income inequality due to limited ownership of resources. Under the present price system of resource allocation, low productivity of capital, low wages, unemployment, and income inequality may persist permanently in the black ghettos because prices, incomes, and the rate of return on capital outside the ghetto make ghetto capital investment among the most profitable firms unattractive and marginal.

In addition, since the ghetto community has only low-paid labor to sell, the ghetto community at present has no way to acquire ownership of capital resources as a means of raising its income. Hence, the operation of the price system dictates a permanent condition of ghetto income inequality that gives rise to the permanent condition of resources being bid away from the ghetto by the rest of the community. The result is a ghetto community of negative capital investment, high cost, rising prices, and easy but expensive credit.

The foregoing analysis suggests that it is not economically feasible for a technologically changing oligopolistic system of pricing and output to absorb a separate labor-intensive ghetto sector through capital investment and employment, either within or outside the ghetto community. Since these strictures upon resources that flow between the black community and the rest of the economy are not self-correcting, consumer spending under the present ghetto economic structure has very little allocational effect upon the employment of capital and labor within the ghetto. That is, consumer spending in the ghetto economy as an economic enclave of retail establishment does not generate capital growth within the ghetto or change the pattern of ghetto resource organization. This implies that black community development must of necessity depend upon a more self-contained and self-directed system of resource flow within the ghetto, and between the ghetto and the rest of the economy.

## Spatial Monopoly Pricing and Low-Income Consumers

We have noted that the poor pay more. This means that on the average the prices of goods and services, particularly consumer durables, and even food prices when quality is considered, are higher in the lower-income black communities than in the higher-income, more affluent white communities. It has been alleged that on the day the relief checks come out in New York City, food prices suddenly go up. Whatever the truth of this allegation, one thing is certain: one rarely finds lower prices in the black ghettos of America. Even the discount houses avoid poor people. How does one explain a higher level of prices in the poverty-stricken areas of the black ghettos? We can account for some of the explanation by looking at the supply side in a determination of individual prices. The supply price of the individual business units in the ghetto is higher due to the diseconomies associated with the small size, the higher cost of capital, the high risk of credit selling to low-income consumers, higher insurance rates, and so forth. But these cost factors on the supply side are determinants that help to make the asking price.

Why is the ghetto consumer willing to pay these higher prices? Why doesn't he go outside the ghetto and buy cheaper? If most ghetto dwellers refused to pay the high prices in the ghetto by shopping outside the ghetto, many high-cost firms would be forced out and perhaps replaced by more efficient firms. But the aggregate gross receipts of ghetto businesses suggests that at least two-thirds or more of ghetto spending is done in the local community. One reason might be the unavailability of credit, especially in connection with the purchase of high-priced consumer durables. A more fundamental reason might be the geographic spatial separation, as well as great social distance between the black community and the white community. So poor black people spend their money where other poor black people do: in the community where they live and meet their friends. This tendency adds a monopolistic element to the supply price of a seller whose product is differentiated in the minds of the buyers on the basis of his location within the black community.

## Major Constraints upon Employment and Output

The Negro sector (black ghetto community) is viewed as a labor export sector (labor intensive) trading a redundant supply of labor for goods in a highly capitalistic (capital intensive) oligopolistic sector. A major constraint on output within the ghetto whose residents produce primarily services (miniscule operations such as small grocery stores, restaurants, bars, barber shops, beauty salons, and the like) is a scarcity of labor-using capital enterprises, together with the required money capital for establishing these specialized types of productive operations, such as small-scale manufacturing concerns. The present small-scale self-employment type of enterprises owned by ghetto residents, as well as the larger white-owned mercantile stores owned by nonresidents, have relatively fixed technical coefficients of production with respect to labor and capital and hire little labor relative to the size of their capital stock. A rise in labor-using capital in the ghetto would raise the marginal productivity of labor now employed in low-paying service-producing industries.

The major constraint on employment in the capitalistic sector is the falling demand in manufacturing industries for the redundant supply of unskilled labor from the labor-intensive black community.

This falling demand and rigid (downward) or rising prices of monopolistically-priced consumer goods in the capitalistic sector causes a decline in the terms of trade between exported black labor from the ghetto and imported consumer goods. For the ghetto living level to rise, capital for manufacturing in terms of the analysis herein developed will be reallocated between the ghetto sector and the capitalistic sector so as to raise the marginal value productivity of unskilled ghetto labor. Therefore, wage rates in the ghetto would become higher than that in the lower-paying service industries outside the ghetto. The wage rate differential favoring the ghetto sector would be due to differences in capital/labor ratios between ghetto manufacturing and lower-paying services industries outside the ghetto. A continuous rise of employment within the ghetto at a higher wage rate would not only help absorb the redundant supply of unskilled labor there, but would ultimately lead to a rise in the price of black labor outside the ghetto, and thereby improve the terms of trade between exported black labor and imported consumer goods from the rest of the economy.

## THE WHITE COMMUNITY AND GHETTO LABOR

In terms of treating black labor as a separate factor of production, the production function for the capitalistic sectors may be written as follows:

$$V = \phi_w(L_w, K_w; t) + \phi_b(L_b, K_w; t)$$

$V$  = annual gross value added
$L_w$ = white labor force
$L_b$ = black labor force
$K_w$ = white capital employed in both sectors and ($t$) refers to the time at which we consider each sector.

$\phi_w$ is the sector in which black labor is underrepresented (Negro percent of given industry employees is less than Negro percent of total industry employees; as, for example, in manufacturing).

$\phi_b$ is the sector in which black labor is overrepresented (Negro percent of given industry's employees is greater than Negro percent of total industry employees; as, for example, personal services).

$\phi_w$ takes on the specific production form: $V_w = w(t) \, L_w{}^l \, K_w{}^k$, where $V_w$ is value added in the first sector and $w(t)$ is the exogenous time trend of increased productivity (technical change). Similarly, value added in the second sector amounts to: $V_b = b(t) \, L_b{}^l \, K_w{}^k$.

Now, the marginal product of white labor is $\Delta V_w / \Delta L_w = lV_w / L_w$. Therefore, the amount received by white labor is $(lV_w / L_w) \cdot L_w = lV_w$. Therefore, the share of white labor in aggregate value added is $lV_w / V$. Likewise, the share of black labor is $lV_b / V$. But since productivity growth in the first sector $w(t)$ is greater than that in the second sector $b(t)$, which is almost stagnant, $V_w$ rises faster than $V_b$. Therefore, the share of white labor in total output rises at the expense of black labor. We next define white labor's share as $l_w = lV_w / V$ and black labor's share as $l_b = lV_b / V$ in aggregate value added. Then, if $l_w$ is 0.63, $l_b$ is 0.04 and $k$ is 0.33, it follows that 0.63 of gross value added will be paid as the wage bill for white workers, 0.04 of gross value added will be paid as the wage bill of black workers, and 0.33 will be paid as aggregate returns to capital. In other words, if the gross national product was $100 million, white workers would receive $63 million, black workers would receive $4 million, and $33 million would go to capital before depreciation.

Our production functions[4] assume that the exponents $k$ and $l$ represent constant fractional shares of value added being received by capital and labor respectively. But since white labor's share $l_w$ gradually rises, black labor's share, $l_b$, falls off even though labor's share $l$ remains fixed. The significance of this is that even if GNP doubled from $100 million to $200 million, labor's share would rise from $67 million to $134 million. However, white workers would *at least* attain, in the aggregate, incomes of $126 million and black workers *at most* $8 million.

In the case of black workers, $l_b = lV_b / V$ would tend to fall over time because black workers are overrepresented in lower-pay-

[4] See M. Bronfenbrenner and P. H. Douglas, "Cross Section Studies in the Cobb-Douglas Function," *Journal of Political Economy* (December, 1939).

ing "constant-returns" service-type industries where there is little possibility of varying the technical coefficients of production. That is, the coefficient of conversion with respect to black labor and white capital would remain constant and, of course, different from that of white-labor capital inputs. Hence, there is little or no change in the marginal value productivity of unskilled black labor. Wage rates in service industries (private household workers, waiters, cooks, hospital attendants, and the like) would tend to remain low. And with a fixed labor-capital ratio under conditions of a redundant labor supply at all levels of capital expansion, there would at any given time be a residual supply of unemployed black labor. Any rise in employment of these workers would be in direct proportion to the rise in the availability of capital for investment in lower-paying service industries where the bulk of low-paid Negroes are employed. But since the rate of returns on capital in these lower-paying service industries is less than that of high-productivity and higher-paying manufacturing industries, the greatest dollar volume of capital expansion would occur in manufacturing. Therefore, as the GNP rises over time, the value of the product ($lV_w$) going to white workers would tend to rise relative to the value of the product ($lV_b$) going to unskilled black workers.

This relative fall in black labor's share will continue indefinitely because of the almost imperceptible shift of the proportion of unskilled black workers out of lower-paying service industries and occupations, as the Negro population increases. The result will be a widening of the dollar gap between black and white workers as shown in Table 4-1. Even if we assume a constant rate of capital expansion in the country as a whole, together with a slower but constant rate of capital expansion in lower-paying service industries, the rate of increase in the black population in urban centers is likely to increase faster than the rate of capital expansion in lower-paying service industries. Again, with fixed $k/l$ ratios, all of these workers could not be employed even at low wages. Under these circumstances, there would be a tendency for the real wage of the great bulk of ghetto residents to equal subsistence based on welfare allowances. For any wage lower than this, the worker would prefer welfare. As a result of this economically fixed wage level, the dollar gap between white and black families would continue to widen.

Table 4-1. Rise in Absolute Gap Between Black and White Family Income, 1964–68

| | (1) | (2) | (3) | (4) | (5) | (6) | (7) |
|---|---|---|---|---|---|---|---|
| Year | Median income of Negro families as a percent of white families | Index of change in white family income 1964 = 100% | Amount of white family income per $100 in 1964 | Amount of black family income per $100 of white family income in 1964 | Absolute gap between black and white per $100 of white (col. 3 minus col. 4) | Index of change in absolute gap | Annual percent rise in absolute difference between black and white family income per $100 of white |
| 1964 | 54 | 100 | $100.00 | $54.00 | $46.00 | 100 | |
| 1965 | 54 | 105.8 | 105.80 | 57.13 | 48.67 | 105.86 | +5.8 |
| 1966 | 58 | 112.5 | 112.50 | 65.25 | 47.25 | 102.72 | −2.7 |
| 1968 | 60 | 130.3 | $130.30 | $78.18 | $52.12 | 113.3 | +10.3 |

Source: (1) U.S. Dept. of Commerce, Bureau of the Census, *Current Population Reports*, Series P-23, No. 29; (2) *Current Population Reports*, Series P-60, No. 72 (Washington, D.C.: U.S. Government Printing Office, 1970).

Thus, over time $l_b$, as both the black labor force and the GNP increase, the proportion of the total income going to black workers will fall relative to the extra income going to the extra white labor force. So the extra income going to the extra white labor force as the GNP rises will not have the same significance for black workers. For example, if the income of black families is 58 percent of the income of white families, and the income of white families is $100, then a rise in the aggregate wage bill, say of 7.3 percent over the previous period would mean a rise of only $4.24 for black families and $7.30 for white families.

Therefore, in the next period, black families would have an income of $62.23, whereas white families would have an income of $107.30, so that the *absolute* gap between the two sets of families is now *wider* by $3.07.

With 41 percent of black families below the poverty level, a widening of the dollar gap between black and white becomes a crucial factor. For it is the absolute amount of the dollar gap (up from 3,300 in 1968 to 3,470 in 1969),[5] not the relative difference between black and white households, that results in absolute ghetto poverty. Furthermore, the relative difference between black and white household median income does not reflect the difference in the average size of black and white families or households. Black households on the average are 16.1 percent larger.[6] Thus, on the basis of difference in family or household size, the absolute dollar gap becomes even larger; a fact obscured by relative differences between their median incomes. How this absolute gap has grown since 1964 is shown in Table 4-1.

As column 5 of Table 4-1 shows, the absolute gap between the median income of black and white families (on the basis of the change in income of black families per $100 of income of white families in 1964) has grown from $46 in 1964, to $52.12 in 1968; an increase of 13 percent. As a result of the rate increase in the income gap, the absolute amount of black family income being lost to white families is growing rapidly, even though the Negro family has received since 1964 a nominally higher proportion of the median

[5] U.S. Department of Commerce, Bureau of the Census, *Current Population Reports*, Series P-60, No. 72 (August, 1970).

[6] U.S. Department of Commerce, *Current Population Reports*, P-60, No. 72.

income received by white families (60 percent in 1969). In 1964, the gap lost in income to black families per $100 of income of white families was $100/$46 or $2.17 of white family income per $1.00 of loss of black family income. In 1968, there was an increase in the rate of gap-lost, amounting to $130.30/$52.12 or $2.50 of white family income per $1.00 of loss of black family income. In 1969, the dollar gap was $2.52 of white family income per $1.00 of loss of black family income.[7] This process of gap-lost is somewhat analogous to a case of two runners in a foot race, where the leading runner is running at a much faster rate and covering a larger distance than the other runner. Naturally, the absolute distance between the two runners will become greater, and will ultimately reduce the slower runner's percentage of the distance covered by the faster runner. This is just what has been happening in the case of black and white family income. That is, the rate of growth in the absolute size of the income gap between black and white families is reducing the rise in the percentage of black family income per $100 of white family income. This is shown in column 7 of Table 4-1, which indicates the annual percentage rise in absolute difference between black and white family income per $100 of white when the growth in the absolute size of the income gap between the two groups is considered. Column 7 shows that between 1964 and 1968 the absolute gap difference shows an annual rise of 5.8 to 10.3 percent, averaging 4.5 percent rise over the period, while column 1, based only on median income shows that the nominal percentage gap difference dropped from 46 to 40 percent, averaging a 4 percentage point drop over the period. Between 1968 and 1969 the relative gap difference did not change, while the absolute dollar gap between black and white family income rose by $175.00, or 5 percent.[8] If the present rate of growth in the absolute size of the income gap continues, we may expect a doubling of the absolute gap difference for 1964 within the next ten years.

In terms of black people's share of aggregate income, we may

[7] U.S. Department of Commerce, *Current Population Reports,* P-60, No. 72.

[8] U.S. Department of Commerce, *Current Population Reports,* P-60, No. 72.

say that the share is decreasing, even though the rate of growth may be higher than that for the white people. That is, the average amount of aggregate income going to the black people has been increasing at a decreasing rate relative to total amount since 1964.[9] In the meantime, the black population is increasing at a faster rate than the rest of the population.

[9] Data exclusively on ratio of Negro to white median family income were not available before 1964.

# Part II

# EFFECTS OF GOVERNMENT POLICIES

As we observed the present state of affairs in the black community in Part I we were able to arrive at the following conclusions. First, the basic problem confronting the black community is the organizational structure of the capital-intensive economy and the economic forces that structure generates. The primary causal factors are technological changes in nonagricultural industries, occurring under conditions of oligopoly, which generate rising prices and a falling demand for unskilled black labor in high-productivity employment. As total output and employment expand under conditions of prosperity we observe the following: (1) a persistently high rate of ghetto unemployment and subemployment, together with low money wage rates; (2) a fall over time in the real income of central city ghettos, together with a continuous rise in the absolute dollar gap between the income of black and white families; and (3) a constant fall in the relative share of aggregate output going to the black community. A decrease in the level of employment in the economy as a whole, accompanied by a curtailment of rising prices, leaves the black ghettos with inordinately high and politically unacceptable unemployment rates.

Second, the present market organization and economic structure of the black ghetto cannot generate significant changes in income and employment of the black inhabitants residing there. The black-owned sector is structurally weak and incapable of expansion; the white-owned sector, which dominates the flow of resources in the black community, is structured to generate an outflow of factor payments to the rest of the economy.

In view of these conclusions, we will examine the effects of some present and proposed governmental policies with respect to the expansion of business and employment opportunities of the black community. Our analysis will be in terms of aggregate or macroeconomic considerations rather than in terms of the microeconomic aspects. This is to say we wish to observe the impact of governmental programs such as black capitalism and employment, manpower, and training programs upon aggregate black community employment and income. Some relevant questions in this connection are: (1) To what extent can the policy of black capitalism add to aggregate income and employment of the black community? (2) To what extent can other policies (employment, manpower, and training programs) reduce the level of unemployment in the black community? (3) Are present and proposed policies really designed to meet the basic economic problem of the black community? (4) Can we expect, in view of the present and some proposed policies, that the black community will continue to experience a high incidence of unemployment in central cities and that a high proportion of the black population will remain in poverty even though their families include full-time, year-round employed workers?

# Chapter 5

# THE EFFECTS OF BLACK CAPITALISM AND MANPOWER PROGRAMS UPON GHETTO EMPLOYMENT AND INCOME

## THE MAINSTREAM HYPOTHESIS

The term *mainstream* has frequently been employed in connection with governmental programs designed to increase business and employment opportunities for the black community, particularly with respect to business opportunities for black capitalists. In the manpower area, amendments to the Economic Opportunity Act to provide for the direct employment of the adult poor in conservation and beautification efforts are officially labeled "Operation Mainstream."

The dictionary defines mainstream as, "the principal or dominant course, tendency or trend." If we apply this definition with respect to business and employment opportunities of the black community, we would expect the policy of black capitalism to place black entrepreneurs in the principal or dominant course of American business. It would also be expected that Operation Mainstream and related manpower programs would bring the pattern of income and employment of black workers into conformity with a general pattern of income and employment of white workers in the economy. We would then have the hypothesis that governmental programs of business and employment opportunities for the black community reduce the differential between business and wage income between black and white people by bringing black people into the principal or dominant pattern of (a) business ownership and (b) wage income and employment.

## A Test of the Mainstream Hypothesis

If the mainstream hypothesis holds with respect to business and employment opportunities for the black community, we should expect the occurrence of the following cause-and-effect relationships due to present policies:

1. That investment by black entrepreneurs under the sponsorship of governmental programs leads to the capture by black capitalists of a rising share of aggregate sales at least in the black community, if not in the customary industry. Also, that this rising share of the market going to black entrepreneurs would have a significant impact upon aggregate employment and income in the black community, if not in the given industry.

2. That the present manpower and training programs would have the effect of reducing the level of black ghetto unemployment, averting the fall in ghetto real income, and closing the dollar gap between black and white families and individuals.

We shall now evaluate the validity of the above hypotheses, which are corollaries of the mainstream hypothesis.

## Can the Present Policy of Black Capitalism Expand the Black-Owned Sector of the Ghetto Economy?

In the last part of Chapter 3 our frame of reference was only the present internal structure of the black-owned sector of the ghetto economy. In this section, we shall consider the capital expansion possibilities of the black-owned sector in terms of the general structure of the ghetto economy as a whole. Our hypothesis is that the ghetto economy as a whole is incapable of growth under its present structure, and that the black-owned sector and the white-owned enclave sector will remain static and in equilibrium with respect to each other. The reason for this static equilibrium condition is found in the existence of a ghetto demand gap referred to earlier (See Figure 3-2). This figure shows that only the white enclave sector can save, but that aggregate savings of these white enclave households flow directly to the outside economy. If the ghetto economy cannot make use of its savings, aggregate ghetto demand will be deficient with respect to new capital investment, and there will be only a replacement demand at best. Since almost no ghetto factor returns are used for purchases in the ghetto, there will always be a general demand gap between aggregate ghetto factor costs and aggregate ghetto factor returns. Empirical evidence for this is shown in Table 3-16 and Figure 3-3, which indicate that 96.9 percent of $215.7 million in ghetto business receipts flow out of the Newark ghetto economy. If almost all business receipts, including that portion of business receipts saved (net of depreciation), flow outside the ghetto economy, neither the white-owned sector nor the black-owned sector can grow. The black-owned sector cannot grow because of its internal structural weakness, and the white-owned sector cannot grow because its enclave structure generates an outflow of factor payments that create a gap between aggregate ghetto factor returns to households and aggregate ghetto demand.

The existence of this demand gap ties changes in aggregate purchases to changes in forces exogenous to the ghetto economy, such as (1) changes in the aggregate real wages of unskilled ghetto labor employed outside the ghetto economy and (2) changes in the per capita amount of relief or public welfare payments. Since (1) and (2) remain rather fixed over long periods of time, we may conclude that market forces within the ghetto tend to freeze the prevailing structural pattern of the ghetto economy. That is to say, there are no endogenous forces within the ghetto economy strong enough to change (1) the marginality of the black-owned sector or (2) the trade-production setup between black labor exports and white enclave imports of consumer goods and services. In addition, given the prevailing production and trade pattern of the ghetto area economics, investments in the ghetto do not lead to the development of the ghetto economy. Such investments merely enrich the outside owners of ghetto resources.

Even if there were a rise in the inflow of wage receipts and welfare payments from outside the ghetto economy such an inflow of purchasing power could not be captured by the narrowly based (see Chapter 3) black-owned sector. As shown in Chapter 3 the black-owned sector of the ghetto economy is not structured to do a large volume of business and/or generate employment. Some indication of the inelasticity of employment with respect to a rise in the predominant type of Negro capital investment in the ghetto is shown by the following statement:

> If black capitalism were even moderately successful over the next decade, it would lead to the creation of between 550,000 and 775,000 jobs. If it achieved even the most optimistic expectations, the new jobs created would account for only slightly more than half of the growth in the Negro labor force. So, in 1980, black capitalists would be able to employ no more than 12 percent (and in actuality probably a much smaller proportion) of the jobs Negroes would need.[1]

In terms of our analysis, the mainstream hypothesis with respect to black capitalism runs aground within the present ghetto market system and economic structure. With a fundamental reshaping, however, of the present ghetto production pattern and resource ownership, a federally aided ghetto development plan could be made highly effective. Such a development plan will be presented and discussed in Chapter 7.

## Can the Present Manpower and Training Policies Reduce the Level of Ghetto Unemployment and Raise the Per Capita Real Income?

We have observed from our analysis of ghetto economic structure that the mainstream hypothesis, though testable, is really not a valid hypothesis in the case of black capitalism. That is to say, the present policies of black capitalism cannot possibly change the present structure of the ghetto economy and these policies really have no bearing on the "mainstream" concept.

[1] Andrew F. Brimmer and Henry S. Terrell, "The Economic Potential of Black Capitalism." Paper presented at the 32nd annual meeting of the American Economic Association, December 29, 1969.

Similarly, we shall undertake to show that although manpower and training programs like black capitalism have had great appeal as antipoverty weapons, they do not pass the mainstream test. That is, manpower and training programs, under peak conditions of prosperity, are incapable of reducing unemployment or raising the per capita real income of the ghetto community.

## PROGRAMS FOR TRAINING AND EMPLOYING BLACK LABOR

The problem is training and employing a permanent and rising annual supply of surplus labor whose real wage rates, without adequate training, cannot rise far above the real wage equivalent of the legal minimum. The large and growing quantity of surplus black labor now depresses real wage rates of black workers near the legal minimum where the legally supported wage rates are accompanied by annual black labor surpluses. The crucial question is: Can present and proposed manpower and training programs wipe out the annual amount of black labor surpluses, considering the fact that during the next ten years there will be an annual net addition to the black labor force of approximately 233,221 workers.[2] If the number trained annually can equilibrate the annual surplus, at what wage will it do so? Will the surplus be wiped out with trained workers receiving the legal minimum wage or a wage rate higher than the minimum because of higher-productivity jobs?

If the annual surplus of black labor is trained and receives only the legal minimum, the result will be continuation of black community poverty. The training program would be converting the unemployed or underemployed poor to the employed poor. For example, the Fair Labor Standards Act requires that a minimum wage of $1.60 per hour be paid for all employment in covered jobs. For all workers newly covered by the 1966 amendments to the Acts, the minimum wage is now $1.45 per hour; but even this minimum increased to only $1.60 per hour by February 1, 1971.

The adequacy of family income, however, depends not only

[2] Computed from *Labor Force Projection by Color, 1970–80*, Special Labor Force Report No. 73, Bureau of Labor Statistics (September, 1966).

upon the hourly wage, but upon the total hours worked during the year and family size. This point has been brought out by the President's Commission on Income Maintenance Programs in November 1969. The Commission states:

> Thus, solving the problem of the "working poor" via the minimum wage becomes a matter of guaranteeing the appropriate number of hours of work to family workers at a sufficiently high hourly wage. The hourly wage that would have to be earned by the heads of nonfarm families of various sizes working 40 hours per week 50 weeks per year in order to lift the family from poverty are:

| Family size | Required hourly wage |
|:-:|:-:|
| 3 | $1.39 |
| 4 | 1.78 |
| 5 | 2.09 |
| 6 | 2.35 |
| 7 | 2.89 |

The Commission goes on to point out that over 60 percent of persons in poor families headed by a nonaged male who worked all year round are in families of six or more.[3]

On the basis of the Commission's computations, the hourly wage required to lift a family from poverty ranges from $1.78 for a family of four to $2.35 for a family of six. All of these rates are above the federal minimum of $1.60 that became effective February 1, 1971.

However, since the federal minimum wage is not geared to family size, and since the families of the poor are generally large, a manpower and training program faces the problem of wiping out labor surpluses at wage rates far above the legal minimum. Do present training and manpower policies meet the problem of black labor surpluses?

## Types of Manpower and Training Programs

Federal manpower and training programs have not been designed to meet the problem of training and finding jobs for a large and

---

[3] Taken by the Commission from the U.S. Department of Health, Education and Welfare, Office of the Assistant Secretary (Planning and Evaluation), Poverty Status Tabulations, 1966.

permanent annual supply of surplus labor customarily employed at low wages. The first federal program aimed at retraining workers was the Area Redevelopment Act, which contained a small training component. The first large training program was the Manpower Development and Training (MDTA) of 1962. This act was an attempt to help workers displaced by industrial location or technological change to meet requirements for unfilled new jobs by retraining them for specific jobs available in local labor markets. The act was never intended to meet the problem of training and finding jobs for large surpluses of unskilled labor. The persistence, however, of large surpluses of black labor in the ghettos of central cities shifted the attention of the MDTA program to the so-called disadvantaged groups. This shift in policy emphasis was reflected in the 1963 and 1965 amendments to the act and in the Economic Opportunity Act of 1964. Included in the Economic Opportunity Act were the Neighborhood Youth Corps, the Job Corps, the adult work experience, and basic education programs. The establishment of the Community Action Program also led to more training opportunities for black workers.

The most recent developments in the manpower training program represent an attempt to make training the disadvantaged a by-product of the operations of existing institutions. The most outstanding example of this is the Job Opportunities in the Business Sector (JOBS) program. This program is cosponsored by the National Alliance of Businessmen and the U.S. Department of Labor. The goal is to induce private employers to hire over 500,000 of the hard-core unemployed by mid-1971. Participating firms provide special services to these new employees and are eligible for federal financial assistance.

Although the JOBS program is limited when compared with the annual increment to the black labor force of 233,000, which will refill in a few years the hard-core level vacated by the 500,000, the acceptance of the concept "hard core" does imply the need for a mass training and employment approach to black labor surpluses.

Without going farther into the details of the various programs under way in different regions of the country, we shall place all of these programs into two broad categories: (1) *structured training programs* and (2) *work experience programs*. Structured training programs provide a formal set of training requirements leading to qualifications for a specific job. MDTA and the Job Corps are the largest of these programs. Work experience programs may be defined as those programs that primarily improve attitudes and general skills by putting enrollees in a working environment under supervised conditions. The Neighborhood Youth Corps is the largest work experience program. The Work Incentive Program, which was designed to improve the employability of welfare recipients, also employs the work experience concept.

## Main Programs

There are three main programs by which government helps or seems to help meet the problem of black labor surpluses in central city slums:

1. Manpower Development and Training: provides institutional and on-the-job training.
2. Job Corps program: provides remedial education, training in job skills, and guidance counseling to disadvantaged young men and women aged 14 to 21 who will require a change in environment in order to prepare themselves for responsibilities of citizenship and to increase their employability.
3. The Neighborhood Youth Corps: three separate but related components are out-of-school, in-school, and summer programs. The in-school and summer programs provide part-time work opportunities for low-income ninth to twelfth graders during the school year and the summer in an effort to encourage them to complete high school. Employers are usually the local school system or other public agencies. The out-of-school system primarily enrolls high school dropouts; the program is expected to provide paid employment, work experience, and other training that will permit them to participate in the competitive job market or will encourage them to return to school.

If we begin with the proposition that unutilized and underutilized black labor surpluses represent a social cost to society as a whole in the way of goods and services not produced by these workers, and that this cost of nonutilization of black labor is borne directly by the black community as an economic loss we are immediately confronted with the question of the most economical way of reducing or eliminating the cost of this loss to the black community.

One way of doing this is to train all subemployed and unemployed workers and place them on full-time year-round jobs paying above the poverty level. To do this is a necessary condition for reducing unemployment and closing the dollar gap between black and white families.

Viewing the economics of the training and manpower programs in this light, we would expect the unemployed labor to be taken off the market, trained, and put back on the market at a higher wage rate. Figure 5-1 shows in graphic form the type of training and manpower model required to raise low-paid and unemployed workers above the poverty level and close the dollar gap.

In Figure 5-1, $OS$ represents the total black labor force, for which there are two labor markets. One labor market is represented

Figure 5-1.  A Training and Employment Model for Unemployed and Low-Paid Black Labor

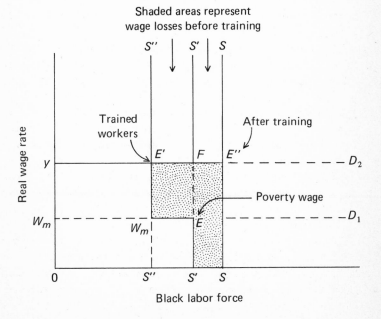

by the supply curve $S'S'$ and the demand curve $D^1$ where $S''S'$ workers are employed at the equilibrium wage $W_m$, at $E$. This market represents a poverty wage level supported by the minimum wage laws. The other market is represented by the supply curve $S''S''$ and the demand curve, $D^2$, where $OS''$ workers are employed at the equilibrium wage shown at $E'$. This market represents a wage level above poverty because the productivity of labor in this market has been increased through training for specific jobs. Falling outside of the two markets, represented by $E$ and $E'$, are the number of unemployed workers represented by $S'S$.

Now, the income loss to the black community due to low wages and unemployment is represented by the areas shaded in red. To eliminate this loss in total wages the model requires abolition of the poverty wage market by: (a) raising the productivity of $S''S'$ workers and $S'S$ workers and (b) transfering these workers to higher wages on the $D^2$ curve.

In terms of Figure 5-1, structured institutional and on-the-job training is the most applicable and effective type. Institutional training provides formal education for skills that can be acquired in less than a year and for which there is continuous local demand. On-the-job training programs are geared to on-site training by employers for specific jobs. We consider these formal and on-the-job training programs economically relevant because they are designed to meet the specific demands of the labor market. We are therefore eliminating so-called work experience programs, primarily designed to improve attitudes and general skills, as not applicable to our training and employment model. It appears that the emphasis is on paying the participants for services performed rather than preparing them for specific jobs outside the program.

The evidence indicates that any pretense at closing the income and employment gap between black and white workers would depend heavily upon a massive application of our training and employment model that is tied specifically to the higher-paying jobs in the labor market. A practical illustration of the miniscule nature of the on-the-job training program for all workers is shown in Table 5-1, illustrating the 1968 statistics of the Manpower Utilization Commission in Philadelphia.

While items 2 and 3 under trainee information show that the average beginning salary per trainee was $68.00 per week, and that

Table 5-1. Statistics of On-The-Job Training Program, 1968

| | |
|---|---:|
| 1. Jobs available | 977 |
| 2. Trainees placed | 928 |
|     Males | 627 |
|     Females | 256 |
| 3. Trainees completed | 801 |
| 4. Trainees terminated prior to completion | 127 |
| 5. Monitor information as of December 1968 | |
|     Trainees still employed by sponsor | 407 |
|     Trainees working in field related to training | 217 |
|     Percentage completed trainees still in | |
|     field for which trained | 77.9% |
| | |
| *TRAINEE INFORMATION* | |
| 1. Number trainees head of household | 422 |
| 2. Number trainees receiving welfare | 15 |
| 3. Average beginning salary per trainee | $68.00/wk. |
| 4. Average salary after completion of training | $92.00/wk. |
| 5. Total salaries paid to trainees while in training | $1,130,919. |
| | |
| *CONTRACT INFORMATION* | |
| 1. Total reimbursements to participating firms | $133,134.08 |
| 2. Average number weeks in training | 11.4 |
| 3. Average training cost per week | $15.00 |
| 4. Average training cost per trainee | $226.29 |

*Source:* (Philadelphia) Manpower Utilization Commission, "On-The-Job Training." Unpublished report, 1968.

the average salary after completion of training was $92.00 per week, there were only 977 jobs available during 1968 in Philadelphia.

## Effects of Structured Training

Four and one-half million persons have enrolled in federally assisted manpower programs between fiscal 1962 and fiscal 1968, and over two-thirds of these enrollments were in work experience programs.[4] Less than one-third (1.4 million) were included in structured programs.

On the basis of average enrollment figures during the period 1962–68, from Table 5-2, Negro enrollees in structured institutional

[4] U.S. Department of Labor, *Manpower Report of the President,* January, 1969 (Washington, D.C.: U.S. Government Printing Office), p. 141.

Table 5-2.   Trainees Enrolled in Institutional and On-The-Job Training Programs (MBTA), August 1962–June 1967

| Characteristic | Institutional program | | | | On-the-job program | | | |
|---|---|---|---|---|---|---|---|---|
| | Total August 1962– June 1967 | July 1966– June 1967 | July 1965– June 1966 | August 1962– June 1965 | Total August 1962– June 1967 | July 1966– June 1967 | July 1965– June 1966 | August 1962– June 1965 |
| Total number (thousands) | 599.5 | 176.5 | 177.5 | 245.5 | 190.0 | 109.9 | 58.3 | 22.7 |
| Percent | 100.0 | 100.0 | 100.0 | 100.0 | 100.0 | 100.0 | 100.0 | 100.0 |
| Race | | | | | | | | |
| White | 65.1 | 59.5 | 62.5 | 70.4 | 76.4 | 75.6 | 76.4 | 79.4 |
| Negro | 32.6 | 37.7 | 35.2 | 27.6 | 21.4 | 21.9 | 21.9 | 17.7 |
| Other | 2.3 | 2.8 | 2.3 | 2.0 | 2.2 | 2.5 | 1.7 | 2.9 |

Source: U.S. Dept. of Labor, *Manpower Report of the President* (Washington, D.C.: U.S. Government Printing Office, April 1968), p. 308.

programs represented about one-third of the enrollment. In on-the-job training programs, Negro enrollees represented about one-fifth of the enrollment. If we assume a Negro unemployment rate of no more than 6 percent of the black labor force, Negro enrollment in structured training programs would be less than 9 percent of the number unemployed. This is shown in Table 5-3. It is noted that on-the-job enrollees per year have represented, over a six-year period, only 1.4 percent of estimated number of Negro unemployed, leaving 91.2 percent of the large pool of unemployed blacks untrained.

Table 5-3.   Ratio of Negro Enrollees in Structured Training Programs to Total Negro Unemployment, 1970

| | |
|---|---|
| Average total Negro unemployed (1970) | 540,000 |
| Percent | 100.0 |
| Average annual enrollment institutional training (1962–68) | 7.4% |
| Average annual enrollment in on-the-job training (1962–68) | 1.4% |
| Not enrolled for specific training | 91.2% |

Source: U.S. Dept. of Labor, *Manpower Report of the President* (Washington, D.C.: U.S. Government Printing Office, January 1969), p. 141.

It is understood, of course, that not all enrollees in structured training programs complete the program, nor are all of them placed in jobs. According to one estimate, 50 percent of all the enrollees have completed their programs and have been placed in jobs.[5] In this case, we may estimate that over a six-year period only a little over 4 percent of the number of unemployed black labor was raised above the poverty level through on-the-job programs.

We conclude that in view of the negligible proportion of the Negro unemployed who are being trained for high-productivity employment, present federally sponsored training and manpower programs will have no significant effects upon closing the dollar gap between black and white families. In fact, we may say that the long-run effects of present training and manpower policies will contribute to a perpetuation of black community poverty by giving the illusion of effective training programs. This is true because the bulk of the trainees are in the "work experience" type of programs, which are (1) specifically designed to get Negroes off relief rolls into poorly paid jobs (for example, the Work Incentive Program) or (2) to get Negroes into low-paying jobs before they get on welfare (for example, the Neighborhood Youth Corps). In either case, the underlying objective is to reduce the costs of welfare by getting Negroes on low-paying jobs rather than to raise the productivity and total wages of the black community.

## Effects of Work Experience Programs

In considering the effects of the work experience training model, remember our basic hypothesis: that the work experience training model is not designed to lift workers out of poverty incomes. A graphic illustration of the model is shown in Figure 5-2.

The shaded area in this figure illustrates the same income loss as shown in Figure 5-1. In that figure, however, we noted that the training program for specific jobs was designed to increase the unemployed and the subemployed to the demand curve $D_2$, which is infinitely elastic at the higher prevailing wage for trained labor. In

[5] *Report of the President's Commission on Income Maintenance Programs*, November 12, 1969 (Washington, D.C., U.S. Government Printing Office), p. 102.

Figure 5-2.  A Work Experience Training Model Continues
Black Ghetto Losses in Real Income

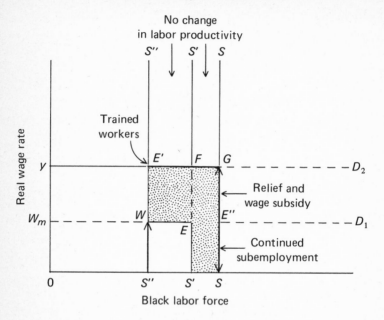

the case of Figure 5-2, there is no plan to raise labor productivity because work experience trainees are assigned to low-productivity employment that pays the poverty wage of $W^m$. Therefore, the objective of the work experience program is to take some portion of the unemployed represented by $S'S$, and place them on the demand curve $D_1$, which is assumed to be infinitely elastic at the low wage $W^m$.

We conclude therefore, that the loss of wage income represented by the shaded area remains pretty much the same after as before "work experience" training, since the subemployed and unemployed, under work experience programs, cannot be shifted to the demand curve $D_2$ where the wage would be at $G$. Part of this gap in income will have to be closed by welfare payments that are likely to take the form of the currently proposed income maintenance plans. We observe that work experience training perpetuates low-productivity employment and welfare payments in the form of income maintenance.

The predominance of the work experience training model is shown by the fact that between 1964 and 1968, over two-thirds of the enrollment in federally assisted manpower programs was in the work experience programs. The Neighborhood Youth Corps is the largest work experience program. This program, as already indicated, has three components: out-of-school, in-school, and summer programs. We have also referred to the Work Incentive Program, designed to improve the employability of welfare recipients.

Emphasis continues upon work experience programs, as shown in the Labor Department's enrollment figures for September 30, 1969.[6] A breakdown of the September figures shows the following participation by program (total = 395,767):

*Manpower Development and Training* (18.9%). Helps unemployed gain new skills and underemployed upgrade skills by training either on the job or in school; 74,759: 35,007 on the job, 39,752 in school.

*Neighborhood Youth Corps* (30.7%). In-school and out-of-school youngsters, to help them stay in school, return to school, or get work experience; 121,500: 89,000 in school and in summer programs, 32,500 out of school.

*Operation Mainstream* (3.0%). Pays older workers in small towns and rural areas to work on public improvement projects; 12,011.

*New Careers* (0.8%). Public service type of jobs leading to careers for poor and unemployed; 3,456.

*Concentrated Employment Program* (17.7%). Provides one-stop service for all manpower and related program services required by area and people most in need; 70,031.

*Job Opportunities in the Business Sector* (7.8%). Government and business work together to hire hard-core unemployed who receive intensive supportive services as they are trained on the job: 30,940.

*Job Corps* (4.4%). Residential program of human renewal and work readiness; 17,697.

Less than 20 percent of the enrollees are in Manpower Development and Training, and only 7.8 percent are in Job Opportunities

[6] U.S. Department of Labor, Office of Information, "News," week of December 1, 1969.

in the Business sector. Almost three-fourths are in work experience programs indicating a substantial rise in the proportion between 1962 and 1968.[7]

In terms of our hypothesis that the work experience model does not offer an escape from poverty, the President's Commission on Income Maintenance Programs reports: The achievements of the 3 million enrollees in these programs vary by program and by locality, but in general, work experience programs tend to place more emphasis on paying for services performed by participants than they do in preparing participants for productive work outside of the program . . . but there is little evidence that a substantial number of work experience enrollees have been prepared for the competitive world by participation in the program.[8]

## CONCLUSION

In summary, we have shown that federal policies in the area of manpower training and employment represent two possible models: One model, represented by Figure 5-1, presupposes the development of black manpower by raising the productivity of employed and unemployed black labor. In practice, this model has benefited only a negligible percentage of the black unemployed through structured and on-the-job training for specific jobs.

The other model, represented by Figure 5-2, presupposes no change in the productivity of labor via training and no change above the minimum wage for the bulk of black labor. The objective of the training program is to reduce the welfare cost by placing workers on low-paying jobs while supplementing their income through some form of income maintenance plan. This model, of course, is not designed to raise the aggregate level of black ghetto wages, which would remain low or at the legal minimum. And, of course, the dollar gap between black and white workers would

[7] U.S. Department of Labor, *Manpower Report of the President,* 1970 (Washington, D.C.: U.S. Government Printing Office), Table 1, p. 59.

[8] *Report of the President's Commission on Income Maintenance Programs,* November 12, 1969 (Washington, D.C.: U.S. Government Printing Office), p. 101.

remain permanent insofar as federal manpower and training policies are concerned.

We have associated this model with so-called work experience programs. It has been the predominant model among ghetto dwellers and is rapidly becoming the most-used model under the Work Incentive Program applied to welfare recipients. When the model is complemented by proposed income maintenance programs under the guise of welfare reform, we observe the following possible results:

The working poor covered under federal minimum wage laws receive, as of February 1971, only $1.60 per hour. Because this is, by definition of poverty wages (below $3,553 for a family of 4), below the poverty level, they would receive a wage supplement to bring income up to the federally defined poverty level. This means that the wage bill of low-wage employers must be supplemented even above the legal minimum. Thus, there will be no incentive or need for low-wage employers to raise wages as long as his workers can get a wage subsidy from the government. If there is no need for employers of the working poor to pay higher than the legal minimum, these workers may never get a raise above the poverty level. If they cannot, 2.9 million working poor families, most of whom are black, will be confronted with the equivalent of a "permanent wage freeze" at the poverty level.

The unemployed poor, instead of being trained for higher-productivity jobs, would be required to register for training and to work under a work experience program where the worker would be assigned to some low-wage job on pain of not receiving the annual income payment. For example, school dropouts would, for the most part, be enrolled in the out-of-school program where they would be assigned to custodial, hospital, and poorly-paid maintenance jobs. They would be paid the minimum wages with very little prospect of increasing their productivity.

The overall result is to perpetuate a large supply of low-wage and low-productivity black workers, with the wage bill of employers held down by federal wage subsidy. This, of course, implies a permanent condition of ghetto poverty and the nonvalidity of the "mainstream" hypothesis.

We conclude that present and proposed governmental policies

(black capitalism; manpower, employment, and training programs; and proposed income maintenance programs) are incapable of dealing with the major forces generating black community poverty. This is so because present policies are geared to the assistance of individuals and families, while the major forces to be dealt with are systemic in origin and must be countered by a systemic approach.

# Part III

# THE SOLUTION

## THE NATURE OF THE SOLUTION

Our analysis in Part II of present and proposed governmental policies indicates that the major forces generating ghetto poverty do not come within the purview of present or proposed governmental programs. These programs—black capitalism, manpower programs, and proposed income maintenance—are tied to the economic assistance of individuals and families rather than to the mass phenomena of ghetto poverty, the inordinate rates of ghetto unemployment, and the fall in the real income of the ghetto economy.

In Part I we saw that the operation of exogenous economic forces (oligopolistic and technological) in the white community have inflicted and continue to inflict external diseconomies[1] upon the black ghettos, the resources of which are primarily labor. These resources have a low income elasticity of demand, as shown by high rates of unemployment in periods of prosperity, while the supply is infinitely elastic at low real wages. We have also observed that factors endogenous to the ghetto market economy, such as the

[1] An external diseconomy is defined as an unfavorable effect on one or more persons that emanates from the action of a different person or firm. See Paul A. Samuelson, *Economics,* 7th ed. (New York: McGraw-Hill, 1967), p. 465.

enclave sector and the land/population ratio of the ghetto, generate forces that restrict the flow of capital to the ghetto economy.

In terms of these two major observations concerning restrictive effects of both exogenous and endogenous forces upon ghetto development, it necessarily follows that removal or counteraction of these forces is clearly indicated. If these restrictive forces cannot be removed without changing the structure of the entire economy, then they should be counteracted by changing the structure of the ghetto economy. Any structural change in the ghetto economy that would counteract or equilibrate these forces would be equivalent to a technological improvement in the ghetto, and would thereby raise the social productivity of the ghetto community. That is, any reduction of external diseconomies in the black community emanating from the white community would result in a reduction of social cost in the economy as a whole, for any given level of factor and product prices. In addition, for any given level of social costs, the result would be a social surplus or gain.

## BASIC QUESTIONS

The tendency toward a fall in the real wage incomes of ghetto dwellers relative to the national output, together with a rise in the dollar gap between black and white families, raises the question of a more productive role for the black ghetto community as a whole in the economic system. If there is a more productive role—one that would cause a rise in black worker productivity and employment— what is this role? What is likely to be the optimum productivity (black community income divided by total man-hours worked) of these workers? What is likely to be the optimum growth rate in their per capita real income; that is, growth rate in black community aggregate income divided by growth rate in black population? How can a change in the industry mix and resource control be brought about so as to counteract to some extent the effects of the black community's low rate of productivity and limited income class mobility as national income rises? How can even the low rate of income class mobility among ghetto workers employed in their present jobs be made to generate capital growth within the ghetto? If there is a rise in the aggregate wage bill paid to ghetto residents employed outside the ghetto economy, how can this addition to aggregate ghetto wages be made to generate capital growth within the ghetto? What is likely to be the capital/output ratio (dollar amount of output per dollar of capital investment) within the ghetto community? How much of the total output will go to ghetto labor? All of these questions ultimately boil down to one basic question: What is the optimum economic relationship between the ghetto economy and the rest of the economy?

That is, as the national income rises, and assuming the continued existence of a rising proportion[2] of black people in central cities, what would be the maximized share of the national income going to ghetto households in the form of factor payments—wages and salaries, dividends, rent, and profits—based upon earnings of ghetto production factors employed inside the ghetto economy and outside the ghetto economy? In order to achieve this optimum condition of income flow between the black and white communities, what would be the economics of restructuring the ghetto economy so as to optimize the distribution of a rising national income among ghetto residents?

## UNDERLYING ASSUMPTIONS

In an attempt to find the answers to the previous questions, the following assumptions are made:

1. That for the indefinite future the great bulk of the black population in urban areas will reside in an all-black community within the core of the central city area, now designated as the black ghetto, and will continue to grow and become an increasingly larger percentage of central city inhabitants.

[2] Between 1960 and 1968, the proportion of Negroes residing in central cities increased from 52 percent to 54 percent, whereas the proportion of whites within central cities dropped from 30 percent to 26 percent. The Negro percentage of the population in central cities rose from 9.5 percent in 1960 to 11.9 percent in 1968, an increase of 25 percent. See U.S. Department of Commerce, Bureau of the Census, *Current Population Reports,* Series P-23, No. 27 (Washington, D.C.: U.S. Government Printing Office, 1969).

2. That technological and economic factors will continue to affect adversely the economic status of workers residing in the ghetto, and that as the size of the ghetto population grows, its relative economic position will deteriorate under present conditions, even if some of the larger firms in the North reduce their present level of race discrimination in employment.

3. That the bulk of the labor force residing in the ghetto is not likely to be shifted en masse from unskilled labor to the category of skilled labor or other high-income employment.

4. That the black ghetto community is a separate labor-intensive economy and will continue to remain so over the long run; and that the bulk of the aggregate received income will consist mostly of low wages and salaries.

5. That the bulk of black workers will continue to reside in the ghetto but work outside of it as exported low-paid labor.

6. That the black power movement as a cohesive and unifying economic and political force in the black community will continue unabated into the indefinite future.

7. That as a result of this black power force there will be a definite trend of government policy toward developing black capitalists in black communities, but the politics and economics of the ghetto community require more than the mere rise of a few more or even many more black capitalists. The economics of the black power case involves the most efficient way of restructuring economic processes within the black community so as to optimize the real income of a redundant supply of black labor residing in the ghetto. Mere substitution of black capitalists for white capitalists under present conditions of resource use is far from an optimum economic condition of ghetto development and growth and could have only minimal effects.

The basic assumptions of this analysis are not, therefore, concerned with the possibility of developing a larger number of black entrepreneurs in the ghetto community. From an economic point of view the color of the entrepreneur is unimportant under the prevailing system of resource allocation within the ghetto. If it were possible for all white entrepreneurs in the ghetto to suddenly turn black, the great bulk of black labor in the ghetto would be no better off than they are now. Furthermore, it is believed that unplanned capital expansion in the ghetto, dependent upon the private initiative of the individual black or white entrepreneur, would have only a negligible effect upon the employment of the bulk of the black labor force residing in the ghetto. Such capital would tend to be mainly invested in relatively small and/or mercantile types of business enterprises functioning as residual employers of a minute percentage of black ghetto labor.

## ECONOMIC AND TECHNOLOGICAL CHOICES

The process of developing a system of resource allocation includes the choice of technology in terms of the ratio of labor to capital, the choice of type and size of enterprise in terms of ghetto consumer demand, and the efficient utilization of scarce black managerial skill available to the ghetto. A problem of such magnitude can hardly be resolved by merely changing the color of the capitalist. Although such a scheme would surely contribute to an increase of black capitalists, it would not affect significantly the economic development of the black community. True economic growth of the black community must be generated by the economic development that implies a change in its economic structure (industry mix) and the resultant change in value added at all stages of production within a circuit system of resource flow.

# Chapter 6

## THE ECONOMIC RATIONALE FOR A SYSTEM OF GHETTO DEVELOPMENT

Development of the black ghetto economy is essentially a problem of restructuring the system of resource organization and control. The ghetto system of market organization of economic processes is delineated from the rest of the economy by spatial, cultural, and economic factors on the demand side for consumer goods. On the supply side, the ghetto economy functions within the general economy as a labor intensive one-sector export economy. Its only export to the rest of the economy is low-priced unskilled labor. Unskilled ghetto labor is traded for goods from the capital-intensive sector of the rest of the economy under conditions where: (1) prices of imports are fixed and rigid (downward); (2) prices of labor (wages) are fixed and rigid (upward); and (3) technological change in the capital-intensive sector acts to reduce over time the economic opportunity for highly paid unskilled labor exports. The combination of these conditions results in deteriorating terms of trade (falling real income) between the black ghetto economy and the rest of the economy, together with high rates of unemployment of unskilled black labor, the demand for which in manufacturing industries becomes increasingly income inelastic relative to the growth rate of the national income.

# ECONOMICS OF BLACK GHETTO DEVELOPMENT

In both industry and agriculture, the effect of technological change has been to increase the available supply of unskilled urban ghetto workers seeking employment. In the urban ghetto areas, the demand for workers has grown less rapidly than the supply, resulting in high rates of unemployment and subemployment. Figure 6-1 illustrates this supply-demand situation. Over time, the demand schedule for unskilled ghetto dwellers as a whole has shifted to the right (increase in the number that will be hired at a given wage), but not as much as the downward shift in the supply schedule. The supply curve is assumed to be perfectly elastic until all workers are employed and relatively inelastic thereafter; hence the tendency of real wage rates among ghetto dwellers as a whole to fall or not to rise above the real wage equivalent of minimum legal wage rate. The increase in the supply of unskilled black workers in urban areas has far exceeded the increase in demand for unskilled black workers under conditions of technological changes in both agricultural and non-agricultural industries (see Figure 6-1).

**Figure 6-1.  Quantity of Unskilled Black Workers
in Central City Ghettos**

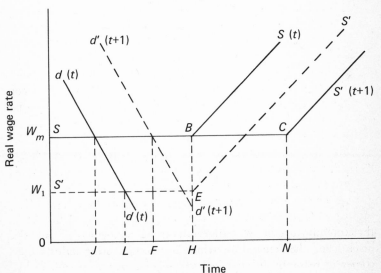

At the minimum wage rate, $W_m$ the demand curve $d(t)d(t)$ and the supply curve $SS(t)$ indicate that only $OJ$ amount of workers will be employed and that $JH$ will be unemployed, assuming that all surplus labor is not exhausted. If there is no minimum wage rate, the real wage rate will fall from $W_m$ to $W_1$. Hence, employment will increase by $JL$, but there will still be $LH$ amount of unemployment. The supply curve for unskilled Negro labor is assumed to be infinitely elastic from $W_m$ to $B$, to $C$, and from $W_1$ to $E$. At $B$, $C$, and $E$ all surplus labor will be exhausted.

Over time, from period $(t)$ to $(t+1)$, the demand curve for unskilled black labor shifts to $d'(t+1)d'(t+1)$ with employment increasing from $J$ to $F$ at the minimum wage $W_m$. But the increase in the supply of black workers from $H$ to $N$, as shown by the supply curve $SS'(t+1)$, far exceeds the increase in demand from $J$ to $F$.

The downward shift of the supply curve from $W_mS$ to $W_1S'$ is drawn on the assumption that the real wage will fall if there is no legal restriction or when supported by the legal minimum. With the accompanying Negro unemployment, money wage rates tend not to rise above the legal minimum. The result is a static condition of both low money wages and low real wages. Under inflationary conditions, the real wage tends to fall.

## Low Wage Rates Tend to Remain Low

This tendency of low wage rates to remain low results in a low rate of income class mobility among ghetto dwellers, thereby resulting in no relative change in the real wage share of the total wage bill going to these workers as the national income changes. The extent of income class mobility among black and white income receivers is shown in Figures 6-2a and 6-2b.

Although the proportion of nonwhite families showed significant movement from lower to higher income classes between 1947 and 1960, the proportion of nonwhite families earning between $3,500 and $5,000 showed very little or no change between 1960 and 1966. And the drop in the proportion of nonwhite families with incomes under $3,000 slowed down while the movement of those just above the poverty level ($3,500 to $5,000) showed little or no change over the six-year period.

Figure 6-2a.  Income Class Mobility of Nonwhite Families
in Constant Dollars, 1947–66

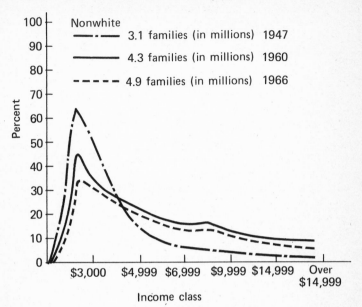

Income class

More recent data (1968)[1] indicate a continuation of limited income class mobility of nonwhite persons below the $5,000 income class. In 1968, 8.3 million nonwhite persons, or 35 percent of the nonwhite population, was below poverty level. In selected central cities taken as a group (New York City, Chicago, and Los Angeles) there was no measurable change in the percentage of nonwhite families below the poverty level over the eight-year period, 1959–67.[2]

In these central cities, however, the number of poor white families declined by an average of one-third.[3] This is reflected in Figure 6-2b, which indicates a continuous rise in the proportion of nonwhite families at all higher income classes for the year 1960 compared with 1947, and for the year 1966 compared with 1960. It should be noted that the bottleneck of income class mobility for white families occurs around $7,000, while the bottleneck of income class mobility of

---

[1] U.S. Department of Commerce, Bureau of the Census, *Current Population Reports,* Series P-23, No. 26; Bureau of Labor Statistics, Report No. 347.

[2] *Current Population Reports,* Series P-23, No. 27  (February 7, 1969).

[3] *Current Population Reports,* Series P-23, No. 27.

Figure 6-2b. Income Class Mobility of White Families in Constant Dollars, 1947–66

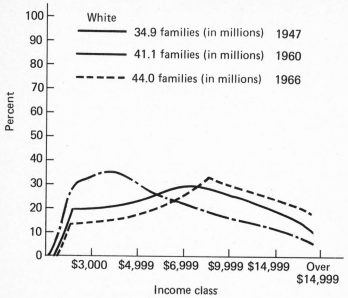

Source: U.S. Dept. of Labor.

nonwhite families occurs around $4,000. This income class mobility bottleneck refers to the point on a family income scale where it is difficult for families to break through. But once the breakthrough comes, the family may move on into higher and higher income classes. To pass through this bottleneck, Negro workers are required to have a college education but white workers are not required to have a college education. However, the chances of a family's presence in the higher income brackets are enhanced if the family head is white, male, and nonfarm, with four or more years of college education.

As a result of the limited income class mobility of workers in the black community, these workers will receive over time a relatively smaller percentage share of the aggregate income. This will occur because under the supply and demand conditions of ghetto labor, that portion of the aggregate wage bill going to ghetto dwellers will not rise proportionately to the rise in the aggregate wage bill for labor as a whole. Also, to the extent that the aggregate real wage bill for labor as a whole fails to rise proportionately to the rise in total output, ghetto dwellers will get a declining share of total output as well as a declining share of that portion of total output going to labor as a whole. The result, of course, will be not only a rising dollar gap between the real income of white families and black families, but also a continuous fall in ghetto worker real income and a rising gap between the growth rates of the national output and the aggregate ghetto real income.

## Systemic Income Inequality

The economics of a system of black community development stems from the problem of systemic income inequality, in which a permanent condition of income inequality is generated by the processes of production and distribution in the economy as a whole. Industrial concentration and oligopolistic pricing and output tend to create monopoly profits and distort the equitable distribution of personal incomes and wealth vis-à-vis the owners of property and the owners of labor.

As shown in Figure 6-3, *DD* is the demand curve and the rising portion of *MC* is the supply curve. The manufacturer halts production at *OX*, when his profits are greatest.

Price is set at *OP*, under conditions of oligopolistic pricing, where restrictions exist on entry, price leadership, tacit agreements, and other price-restraining measures. It should be noted that monopoly profits rise, as shown by the cross-hatched area, and that the rise of such monopoly profits distorts the share of total factor payments going to labor.

As a result of the process of production and distribution under oligopolistic pricing, there is a tendency for labor's share of the national income to remain static over time and perhaps even fall in the short run under conditions of automation. Figure 6-4 shows an estimate of labor's share as being currently 75 percent of the national income, together with the dotted line indicating a possible short-run fall in the proportion going to labor under conditions of automation.

Figure 6-3.  An Illustration of Oligopolistic Pricing

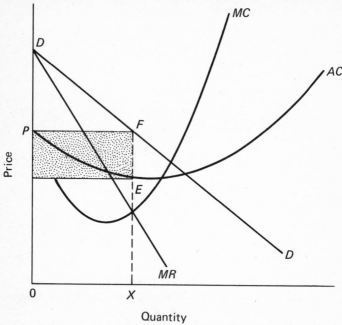

It is also likely that a fall in labor's share under conditions of automation may remain permanent—depending, of course, upon the ability of labor unions to obtain wage raises proportionate to the rise in productivity. It is still an open question as to whether labor unions have made a permanent change and/or can make a permanent change in the proportion of the national income going to labor as a whole.

## GHETTO DEVELOPMENT AND SYSTEMIC INCOME INEQUALITY

Since the incidence of systemic income inequality is heaviest in the black ghettos, the approach to the problem of ghetto development must be designed to counteract or eliminate the effects of systemic inequality upon the ghetto community. The magnitude of the prob-

Figure 6-4.  Allocation of Income Between
Labor and Capital
National Income = 100%

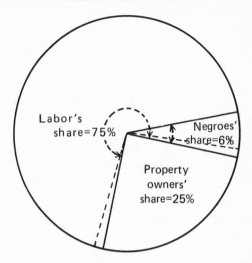

lem of systemic income inequality, the effects of which a ghetto development system must face, is shown in the following table:

| Percent of people | Percent of income |
|---|---|
| 20% | 5% |
| 40 | 16 |
| 60 | 32 |
| 80 | 55 |

While the lower 20 percent of the people receive only 5 percent of the income, the upper 20 percent receive 45 percent of the income. It is not surprising that 13 million families, or 25 percent of the total families whose incomes are $10,000 and over, buy half of the nation's output. Now, if the upper 25 percent of the families get half of the "economic pie," who is able to buy the other half? Well, the lower 20 percent of the people can buy only 5 percent, the lower 40 percent can buy only 16 percent and the lower 60 percent can buy only 32 percent because they receive only one-third of the income. This means then that two-thirds of the economic pie must be bought by those among the upper 40 percent of the population.

What does this type of distribution of income and purchasing power tell the business man in making his decision as to:

1. What to produce?
2. How much?
3. In what proportion?
4. For whom?

The answer is obvious. The bulk of the output in terms of type of goods produced, proportions, and prices, is geared to the $10,000-and-over income class who buys half of the goods. For example, a private builder would decide to produce houses selling for $30,000 and up. Very few, if any, houses would be constructed for ghetto dwellers or for those who can afford to pay only $15,000 or $20,000. And of course, the lower 20 percent of the population with only 5 percent of the income would be forever consigned to the slums and some of the lower 40 percent of the population with only 16 percent of the income would be consigned to the old, high upkeep houses in the central cities that have been sold by the more affluent 25 percent of the families who move to the suburbs.

A ghetto development system, therefore, must face and seek to counteract a serious condition of income inequality in an economy where economic processes allocate the bulk of produced resources to the more affluent minority within the economy.

## PERMANENT INCOME INEQUALITY: A HYPOTHESIS

Under present conditions of resource organization within the economy as a whole, we may generalize by saying that the black community confronts a general economy with a built-in and permanent condition of income inequality and relative poverty among substantial segments of the population. Our hypothesis is that an economic system that allocates the bulk of its resources to the more affluent minority of the economy generates further income inequality and perpetuates a permanent income gap between the richest and the poorest sectors. As incomes and profits rise, the poorest sector of the economy does not share proportionately with the more affluent sector in the rise of incomes and profits. Further income inequality and more relative poverty result.

## Examples of Income Gap Hypothesis

An extreme example is the relatively fixed disparity between the median income of black families, upon whom the incidence of inequality and poverty falls heaviest, and the median income of white families. Just as the unemployment gap between black and white families has averaged about 2 to 1 since 1948, the income gap between white and black families has averaged approximately a 2 to 1 ratio despite year-to-year changes above or below the 2 to 1 ratio. These annual changes in ratio are shown in Figure 6-5. It should be

**Figure 6-5.  Black and White Median Income, 1950–67**

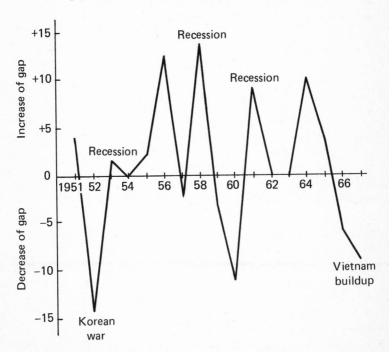

*Source:* Based on data of the U.S. Dept. of Commerce, Bureau of the Census, *Current Population Reports,* Series P-50, No. 51 (January 12, 1967).

Figure 6-6.  Parity Price Ratio Curve

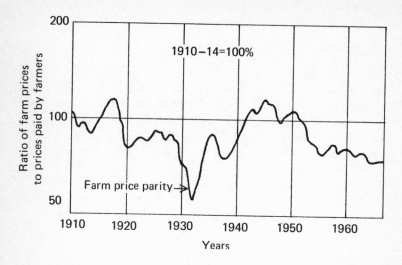

noted that the changes in the black/white income gap are influenced by cyclical factors as well as by the war and inflation. But the main point is that over time, there is no trend toward a reduction of the gap. Thus, the white/black income ratio appears to be permanent even in periods of peak prosperity.

Another example of permanent income inequality between the richer and poorer sectors of an economy is the income inequality between the farm and nonfarm population. For the last 60 years, the "farm gap," like the "Negro gap" has persisted, notwithstanding farm price support, acreage restrictions, and other governmental farm subsidies. This income gap continues because the real income of farmers depends heavily upon the terms of trade between competitively priced farm goods and oligopolistically priced nonfarm goods. Therefore, the ratio of prices received by farmers for farm produced goods to prices paid by farmers for nonfarm goods is a measure of the real income gap between the farm and nonfarm producers.

In Figure 6-6, the parity-price ratio curve shows that except in periods of war the farm gap remains permanent. In the world economy, we observe this same phenomenon of income inequality between the rich and poor countries,[4] and the existence of a permanent and growing income gap between the rich and poor countries.[5]

## Reasons for the Income Gap

The existence of a permanent condition of income inequality—a growing income gap between the rich and poor sectors of a national or world economy—is to a great extent due to oligopolistic market forces that generate a deterioration in the terms of trade between the rich and poor economic sectors. That is, the richer sector is characteristically more oligopolistic in pricing and output, while the pricing of salable resources of the poorer sector is more in line with the pure competitive model. This is certainly true of unskilled black ghetto labor, which represents the main salable resource of the black community. The supply curve of black labor is infinitely elastic at the prevailing wage for unskilled labor, and as we have seen, technological changes have lowered and will continue to lower the demand for unskilled black workers. So, if the black community has mainly an infinitely elastic supply of unskilled labor to sell, there will be a growing disparity between the prices paid by the black ghetto for monopolistically priced consumer goods and the prices (wage rates) received for unskilled black labor.

Similarly, if the supply curve for farm commodities is relatively inelastic, the prices the farmer will receive for a relatively inelastic supply of goods priced under competitive conditions will continue to be disproportionate to prices that the farmer must pay for monopolistically priced goods.

In the case of the poor sectors of the world economy, the trade of primary products for industrial goods between the poor sectors and the developed sectors represents the same phenomena of terms of trade deterioration and income gap.

[4] Seventy percent of the world population (Asia, Africa, and Latin America) receive 20 percent of the world income. The United States, with 6 percent of the world population, receives 30 percent of the world income; and Western Europe, with 9 percent, receives 22 percent of the world income. Paul A. Samuelson, *Economics,* 7th ed. (New York: McGraw-Hill, 1967), p. 736.

[5] Paul Prebisch, *Toward a New Trade Policy for Development* (United Nations Conference on Trade and Development, 1964); Hans Singer, *International Development: Growth and Change* (New York: McGraw-Hill, 1964).

Perhaps the most pervasive market force, on the demand side, underlying the deterioration in terms of trade between the poorer and richer sectors of an economy is the income inelasticity of the demand for poorer sector resources. In the case of the black community, the salability of unskilled black labor does not rise proportionately to the rise in industrial output. In fact, the ratio of unskilled labor to capital tends to fall in manufacturing industries and the labor/capital ratio in service industries tends to remain constant.

For agricultural products and for primary products from underdeveloped countries there is a high degree of income inelasticity of demand. Expansions of output and incomes in the richer sectors of the world do not lead to a proportionate rise in the quantities demanded of agricultural and other primary products. Hence, when incomes rise, the percentage of income spent on these commodities tends to fall.

We may conclude then, that in terms of our examples, the income gaps between richer and poorer sectors remain permanent because of: (a) disparity in price ratios between oligopolistic markets and pure competitive markets; and (b) the income inelasticity of demand for the salable resources of the poorer sector. The economic result is that the receipt of income in the poorer sector constitutes a falling percentage of the rising incomes of the richer sector. Hence, the permanent gap continues.

It must be recognized, of course, that the extremity of the economic gap in the black ghetto case is highly aggravated by racial factors such as discrimination in employment, housing, and education. It is the basic way in which the economic system functions, however, both on the national and international level, that generates poverty and inequality, nationally and internationally, as total output rises. We may say here, parenthetically, assuming no serious modification of the way incomes are distributed in the U.S. economy, that although we now have the beginning of a revolt against poverty conditions by the poor black community, within a decade or so we may have a revolt of the poor white against "poverty in the midst of plenty." Sooner or later the poor black and the poor white may come to recognize the similarity of their economic interests. Let us go back to our hypothesis that under conditions of income inequality, rising incomes and profits generate further inequality and perpetuate a permanent gap of inequality and relative poverty. Our empirical evidence for this hypothesis is based upon differentials in income class mobility among various income groups as the total output of the economy expands. Data on income class mobility is shown in Table 6-1. Observe that in 1955 24 percent of U.S. families and individuals had incomes under $3,000. This figure was 17 percent by 1965, representing a drop of 29.2 percent over a period of ten years —a compounded rate of nearly 3.4 percent per year. In other words, taking under $3,000 as a poverty level, only three out of 100 families and unrelated individuals below the poverty level rose above the poverty level each year over a ten-year period. Since in a constantly expanding economy poverty must be viewed in relative terms rather than in terms of a fixed level of subsistence, we cannot regard a constant and fixed basket of real goods purchasable for the equivalent of $3,000 in constant dollars as an all-time level of escape of families from poverty. As the economy expands, the amenities of life change, tastes change, social necessities change, and a fixed basket of goods regarded today as being above the poverty level will be below the poverty level tomorrow. So, if we regard poverty in relative terms, we must compare the relative income class mobility of the poor with that of higher-income groups. In this respect we observe that the big mobility in income class is taking place among families and individuals going into the $7,000 to $9,999 income class,

**Table 6-1.**  **Distribution of Income of Families and Unrelated Individuals, Showing Index of Change by Income Class, 1965, 1960, and 1955**
(Under $3,000 = 100%)

| Income class | 1965 | | 1960 | | 1955 | |
|---|---|---|---|---|---|---|
| | Families | Index | Families | Index | Families | Index |
| Under $3,000 | 17% | 100.0% | 20% | 100.0% | 24% | 100.0% |
| $3,000–4,999 | 16 | 94.1 | 19 | 95.0 | 24 | 100.0 |
| $5,000–6,999 | 18 | 106.0 | 22 | 110.0 | 24 | 100.0 |
| $7,000–9,999 | 24 | 141.2 | 21 | 105.0 | 18 | 75.0 |
| $10,000–14,999 | 17 | 100.0 | 13 | 65.0 | 8 | 33.3 |
| $15,000 and over | 8 | 47.0 | 5 | 25.0 | 2 | 8.3 |

*Source:* U.S. Dept. of Commerce, Bureau of the Census, *Current Population Report, Consumer Income,* Series P-60, No. 51 (Washington, D.C.: U.S. Government Printing Office, 1967).

into the $10,000 to $14,999 income class, and particularly into the $15,000 or over income class. In this respect, in 1955, for every 100 persons in absolute poverty (under $3,000) there were 75.0 in the $7,000 to $9,999 income class. In 1960 there were 105.0 and in 1965 there were 141.2. That is, taking those in poverty as representing a base of 100 in each of the given years, the index of change for those in the $7,000 to $9,999 income class relative to those in the poverty class rose from 75.0 to 141.2 over a ten-year period. Similarly, for every 100 families and individuals in poverty in 1955, there were 33.3 in the $10,000 and over income class, 65 in this class in 1960, and 100 in 1965. This shows that relative to those in poverty the index of change of those in the $10,000 and over income class rose from 33.3 in 1955 to 100 in 1965.

While income class mobility among those going into the $7,000 and above income classes (relative to those in poverty) has shown fantastic changes since 1955, families and unrelated individuals just above the poverty level have shown very little change. In fact, the movement of families and unrelated individuals into the $5,000 to $6,999 income class relative to those in poverty has become increasingly less since 1960. Relative to the number of families in the poverty group, the number of families and unrelated individuals moving into the $5,000 to $6,999 income class fell from 110 for every 100 below $3,000 in 1960 to 106 in 1965.

## CENTRAL CITY PROSPERITY: A THEORY OF MAINTAINABLE EFFECTIVE DEMAND

Income inequality, with its incidence falling heavily upon a large and growing proportion of a ghetto population located in the heart of central city, is bound to generate a general problem of maintainable effective demand in urban communities. Low incomes among a substantial percentage of the urban population set limits beyond which consumer spending cannot rise, even including consumer credit. In terms of the acceleration principle,[6] consumer spending cannot level off without having a downward effect upon capital

---

[6] The accelerated effect of a change in consumption on investment levels. Consumption has to keep increasing in order for investment to stand still. A fall in the rate of consumption reduces the level of net investment.

expansion. Thus, a large and growing community of poor black people in the heart of central cities creates conditions of economic instability because of the slow rate of rise of low incomes, thereby further accelerating conditions of unemployment and poverty.

These effects are derived from the following hypotheses.

*Hypothesis 1.* Under conditions of income inequality in a developed capitalist economy, self-sustaining output or maintainable consumer spending depends heavily upon the mobility rate of income classes (the rate at which families and individuals move from any given low income class to a higher income class). For the ghetto, which consists largely of people who have only their labor to sell, the crucial dependent variable is income received.

We see the relationship between mobility and income in Figure 6-7, where mobility $(M)$ determines the level of income $(Y)$ that can be attained and sustained by the ghetto dweller. The curve rises sharply throughout its length, indicating that at extremely low levels of mobility relatively less income is attainable. At higher levels

Figure 6-7.  Relationship of Mobility and Income

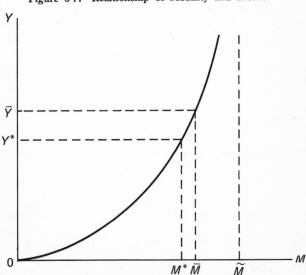

of mobility, however, the income/mobility ratio is greater, and the absolute level of income attainable is larger. The amount of sustainable income at the level of mobility $M^*$ is $Y^*$. If mobility now rises to $\overline{M}$, sustainable income rises by a larger amount, to $\overline{Y}$. If we call $(\overline{M} - M^*)$, $\Delta M$ and likewise call $(\overline{Y} - Y^*)$ $\Delta Y$, then the ratio $\Delta Y/\Delta M$ is the slope of the curve. It represents the rate at which changes in the level of mobility cause changes in the level of sustainable income. We see that it is positive, so that a rise in the level of mobility is always followed by a rise in the level of sustainable income. However, we also know that the curve rises at an increasing rate. We may therefore say that $\dfrac{\Delta 2_y}{\Delta 2_m}$ is positive.

Throughout the above analysis, we have assumed that income and output are (a) equal and (b) at the maximum sustainable level. We therefore assume that (a) prices are stable and (b) full employment of all resources prevails in the economy.

We also have a maximum level of mobility given to us $(M)$ by structural considerations. Our mobility-income curve approaches $M$ asymptotically, touching it only for an infinitely large level of income.

*Hypothesis 2.* The relationship between family consumption and total value of output (net of depreciation and taxes) will depend on the rate of growth of family income relative to the growth of output. If the total value of output grows faster than family income, overall consumption will fall relative to total output. The rise in family consumption, therefore, will depend not as much on the absolute level of aggregate income as on the relative rise in family income in relation to the aggregate, which will depend on the mobility rate of income classes.

This is shown in Figure 6-8. The 45° line is the break-even line between consumption $(C)$ and income $(Y)$. At any point on this line we have family consumption as equal to income. $C^*$ is the minimum level of consumption that a family considers necessary for itself. This need not be a physical minimum. It may very well be a social minimum, dictated more by the demands of society than those of economic need. At this point, our family earns no income and spends the amount $OC^*$. As its income rises, consumption rises very gradually until the break-even point is reached $(\overline{C})$. Here, con-

Figure 6-8.  Relationship of Consumption to Income

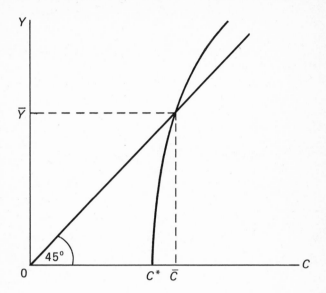

sumption is equal to income, and our family neither saves nor dis-saves. At points to the right of $\bar{C}$, the family begins to save. We may therefore break up the graph into regions of saving (points above the 45° line) and regions of dissaving (points below it). Our theory is largely Keynesian. However, the exceedingly steep slope of the consumption function to the left of $\bar{C}$ is logically deduced from the fact that families consider a certain minimum level of living essential irrespective of income earned in the corresponding period of time.

One minor point should be made at this stage. Our consumption function is a psychological schedule. It states what families would consume out of given levels of income at any point in time. Families cannot stay on the schedule to the left of $\bar{C}$ forever. The evidence indicates, however, that some families do have consumption levels lower than $\bar{C}$ all the time. This can be explained if one accepts the view that low-income families "take turns" dissaving, so that large numbers of families are not forced into bankruptcy. The break-even point for family consumption and income according to our data is around $15,000 per annum, which in 1965 covered over 90 percent of all U.S. families. We now graph our third postulate. It is represented in Figure 6-9.

The graph merely illustrates the fact that one determinant of mobility levels is level of family consumption. This relationship is subject to a maximum attainable level of mobility, $M$. The maximum level may be attained for a finite consumption level, $C$. This is shown as the curve (2).

*Hypothesis 3.*  The mobility rate of income classes depends on the rate of movement of workers from lower-paying industries to higher-paying industries, from lower-paying jobs to higher-paying jobs, or from lower-paying geographic areas to higher-paying areas. This rate of industrial, occupational, and geographic mobility of labor, however, will depend primarily on the rate of sustained expansion in output.

In the final analysis, the mobility rate of income classes depends ultimately upon the sustained rate of increase in output. A sustained

Figure 6-9.  Relationship of Mobility to Consumption

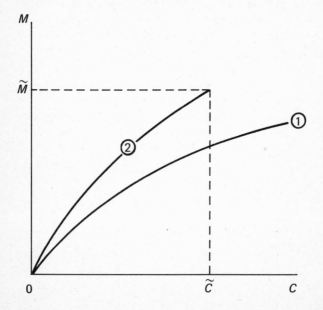

rise in output, however, depends on a sustained rise in consumption, particularly the consumption of big-ticketed items such as consumer durables, of which a fall in consumption represents the first indication of an overall deficiency in consumer purchasing power. Since an increase or decrease in the mobility rate of income classes is directly associated with the mobility rate of labor that is associated (in terms of consumption) with an increase or decrease in the aggregate wage bill, we may say that changes in the aggregate wage bill in its relation to total output represent the crucial factor in maintainable effective demand.

We are substituting here for the Keynesian notion of the propensity to consume and the marginal propensity to consume what may be called the incremental-consumption-income ratio, which is conceived of as a function of the ratio of the rise in aggregate wages to the rise in aggregate income. That is to say, the incremental-consumption-income ratio is conceived of as a direct function of the incremental wage-income ratio. The percentage rise in aggregate consumption relative to the percentage rise in aggregate income is a function of the percentage rise in aggregate wages relative to the percentage rise in aggregate income. The Keynesian notion that the marginal propensity to consume falls or the marginal propensity to save rises as the aggregate income rises is applicable for the whole economy. This concept does not deal with that portion of the economy where incomes are in the neighborhood of subsistence level. First, any increase in income (as a result of wage bill increase) will go directly to consumption as low-income families, theoretically, have high propensity to consume.

Second, the Keynesian theory of marginal propensity ignores the income distribution aspect and provides no information as to how the incremental aggregate income will be distributed. For example, in the United States in 1965 only 8 percent of the families and unrelated individuals received an income of $15,000 or more. Evidence shows that for income classes up to $15,000, there is no significant fall in the proportion of consumption out of additional income. We can say, therefore, that for over 90 percent of U.S. families, there is no significant rise in the schedule of savings as income rises. The saving propensities of urban consumers are not in accordance with the Keynesian idea that attributes a fall in consumption to a rise in a marginal propensity to save. Thus, the rise in new investment in urban communities is more the function of the *incremental-wage-income ratio* where the rise in schedule of savings occurs among a small percentage of consumer spending units.

Since that proportion of the total value of output, net of depreciation and taxes, representing family income and consumption, is part of the aggregate supply price of consumer goods (wages plus profits) of the given output, any deficiency in family income and consumption relative to the aggregate supply price of consumer goods is due to a rise in total profits disproportionate to the rise in total wage bill. That is to say, for any given schedule of new investment, if we let the aggregate supply price of consumer goods equal $S_p$, where $S_p = W$ (wages) plus $P$ (profits) or total value of output, and if we let total family consumption equal $C_w$ (assuming that more or less all or about 90 percent of the families spend almost all of their income on consumption, and that almost all of the family income is from wages and salaries) then, if wages rise proportionately to profits, the percentage increase in wages would equal the percentage increase in the supply price of consumer goods, which would equal the percentage increase in consumption out of wages. But, if the percentage increase in the supply price of consumer goods is greater than the percentage increase in wages, then the percentage increase in profits would be greater than the percentage rise in wages relative to profits, and hence a deficiency in consumption would occur due to the disproportionate rise in profits relative to wages.

We may say, then, that a self-sustained rate of rise of output in a capitalist economy under profit conditions that generate income inequality depends upon: (1) the relation of the rise in aggregate wages to the rise in the aggregate supply price of consumer goods; (2) the income class mobility rate on which depends the overall rise in the aggregate wage bill and the rate of rise in the aggregate wage bill relative to total profits; and (3) the extent of the deficiency in family consumption for any given rate of new investment due to differences in the relative rates of change between wages and profits. If the relationship between profits and wages is held constant as output expands, that is, if the percentage rise in wages is equal to the percentage rise in profits for any given rise in the supply price of consumer goods, then the percentage rise in wages, where the percentage rise in wages is equal to percentage rise in consumption, will maintain the current rate of rise in new investment by maintaining the rate of rise in the supply price of consumer goods. Hence, there is no overall deficiency in family consumption. This is the essence of our theory of maintainable consumer spending in urban communities *under conditions of monopoly profits and income inequality.* That is, if total effective demand in our urban communities is defined as replacement demand, plus new investment, plus the demand represented by the existing wage bill, plus the rise in the total wage bill where all wages are spent, we may say that the amount of the rise in investment with respect to the amount of rise in income is proportionate to the amount of the rise in wage consumption with respect to the amount of rise in income, where the percentage rise in wages equals the incremental-consumption-income ratio. Or, we may say that the incremental-investment-income ratio is equal to the incremental-consumption-income ratio, which is equal to the incremental-wage-income ratio.

A rise in effective demand may then be defined as the rise in the level of profits with respect to a given level of investment, plus the amount of rise in aggregate wage bill, where the rise in profits represents the difference between the amount of the rise in total revenue minus the amount of the rise in total wages for a given level of investment. Since the rise in profits represents the rise in the ratio of profits to investment, we may designate this relationship as the profits-investment ratio, or as the savings-investment ratio, assuming that incremental profits are for the most part saved and not spent on consumption. This assumption would be consistent with the Keynesian idea of the marginal propensity to save at the highest income level.

Now, the rate of rise in investment is greater than the rate of rise in profits for any given level of investment, where the rate of rise of investment is a function of the rate of rise in the wage bill. This occurs if the incremental-consumption-income ratio is equal to the incremental-wage-income ratio, where the incremental-wage-income ratio is proportionate to the aggregate-wage-income ratio. Since we have already equated the rise in profits for any given level of investment with the rise in savings for that level of investment, the rate of rise in investment is greater than the rate of rise in profits.

The rise in investment is also greater than the rise in savings. That is, under conditions where the incremental-consumption-income ratio is proportionate to the aggregate-wage-income ratio, the rate of rise in investment will exceed the rate of rise in savings as well as in profits.

This occurs because the incremental-consumption-income ratio, which equals the incremental-wage-income ratio, holds the profits-savings-investment ratio constant for any given rise in investment with respect to the rise in income. Under such conditions, investment rises proportionately to the rise in consumption, which is a function of the absolute amount of rise in the wage bill for the given level of employment. A rise in the profit-savings-investment ratio for a given level of employment is proportionate to the rise in the wage bill relative to the rise in income. If the wage bill for a given level of employment rises proportionately to the rise in income, the ratio of profits to income will remain constant while the wage bill for a given level of employment rises proportionately to the rise in income, and the profits-savings-investment ratio will also remain constant. In other words, entrepreneurs will receive a constant rate of profits from a constant rise in consumption proportionate to the rise in the wage bill.

We conclude, then, that in a world of poverty and income inequality side by side with wealth and luxury, the problem of avoiding economic instability and unemployment is essentially a problem of maintaining equality between the rate of rise in profits and the rate of rise in wages. When the ratio of profits to investment rises for any given level of employment and income without a corresponding percentage rise in the wage bill for that level of employment and income, there is a fall in consumption and investment for that level of income. In other words, the rise in profits for the given level of investment becomes greater than the rise in total income, and this condition results in a fall in aggregate wages relative to the rise in total income. It is the fall in the aggregate wage bill relative to total income that causes a fall in investment at that level of income relative to the rise in profits. That is, the percentage rise in investment is less than the percentage rise in profits where a rise in profits for a given level of investment results in a fall in the amount of wage increase relative to the increase in income. This leads to a fall in the amount of consumption relative to the rise in income, thereby reducing the rise in investment with respect to the rise in income.

## The Theory

We are now in a position to set out the theory in skeleton form on the basis of the assumptions underlying our model. (See Part III, introduction.) In the last section we have added economic postulates to these fundamental assumptions. Figure 6-10 presents a diagrammatic representation of the theory.

The figure depicts Figures 6-7, 6-8, and 6-9 in parts (a), (b), and (d). Part (c) is merely a device to transfer the level of mobility

Figure 6-10. Relationship of Mobility, Income and Consumption

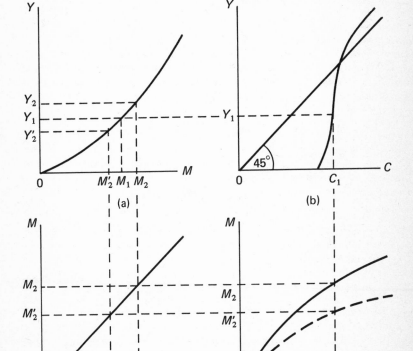

from the condition of determined variable in an $e$ time period to that of the explanatory variable in the next time period.

Our system works as follows: We start out with a *given* level of mobility in time period one, say $M_1$. This determines the maximum sustainable level of income, $Y_1$. We carry this amount over into part (b) and derive the level of consumption obtainable by a family attaining this level of income. This is $C_1$. We now move into part (d) and likewise determine the new level of mobility $M_2$. We can now trace through part (c) the level of income in the next time period, $Y_2$. If $Y_2$ is greater than $Y_1$, we know that the family chosen has a growing level of income. If it is less than $Y_1$, we know that the income level is falling. The family is struggling to survive. In between, we have a stagnated level of income, which is possible at either a high or a low level of income.

In the graph shown, a family that dissaves has a chance to get past the break-even point and will do so in the third time period. The three schedules make for growth. If one of them is changed, however, it can easily be shown that a family that dissaves will gradually be obliterated. Let the schedule in part (d) be changed from the solid line to the dotted one. Then, for an initial level of mobility, $M_1$, we determine a new level $M'_2$, which is less than $M_1$. The family earns decreasing levels of income until its income falls to zero.

The interesting feature of such a theoretical scheme is that it enables us to segregate an economy into a variety of family incomes, some of which may be rising while others may be falling or stagnant. One may look upon a ghetto economy that is trapped in the dissaving level of income while the nonghetto part may be steadily growing. It is possible in such a scheme to have a growing divergence between the two groups of families.

## The Application of Aggregate Demand Theory to Black Ghetto Development

In applying our theory of maintainable income to the urban community vis-à-vis the black ghettos, a major problem of the urban community is to raise the aggregate wage bill of the black ghettos proportionately to the rise in profits and income in the urban community as a whole. This is a necessary condition of maintainable income in the urban community as a whole because income class immobility and income inequality in the black ghettos create deficiencies in the aggregate wage bill of the urban community as a whole, thereby resulting in a fall in the level of investment. Now, because of the pattern of employment of black workers in low-wage and low-productivity jobs it is not likely that a rise in aggregate wage bill of the black ghetto will occur as a function of the rise in profits and income in the urban community as a whole. But the deficiency in aggregate wage bill of the black ghettos can be made up out of profits earned in the black ghettos. This could be achieved by transferring to the black community as a whole community ownership of all private capital resources located in the black ghettos. This would give the black community as a whole a right to the whole product of their community.

The black ghetto's right to the whole product of its community means that profits would go directly to the black ghetto as a result of employing its own resources, rather than through transfer payments in the form of welfare receipts. These welfare payments represent an attempt to make up deficiencies in the aggregate wage bill through the redistribution of higher incomes and profits from the more affluent to the poverty-stricken black community. This is a socially more costly way of maintaining the level of spending and income in urban communities. Everybody would be better off and no one would be worse off if all privately owned capital resources of the black ghettos were purchased outright and transfered to the black ghettos; this would be a business transfer payment rather than a social transfer in the form of welfare payments. Furthermore, it would be infinitely more economical and socially more significant if, instead of making piecemeal loans in the black community to initiate small marginal enterprises, one huge loan would be made to a holding company operation with controlling interest in all capital resources in the black ghettos. The risk would be spread over all enterprises operating in the black ghettos, and uneconomic and marginal enterprises would be replaced with more efficient and optimum-sized units. Furthermore, high caliber management could be afforded for the top positions in one big corporation owned by the black community and providing goods and services to the residents of such a community in each of the major cities throughout the United States.

The economic justification for maximizing total output and profits in the black community, under conditions where the people of the black community receive the whole product, is based upon our hypothesis that the relationship between family consumption and total value of output (net of depreciation and taxes) will depend on the rate of growth of family income relative to the growth of total output. If the total value of output in the urban community as a whole grows faster than family income in the black ghetto sector, overall consumption will fall relative to total output. Overall consumption will fall because under conditions of income inequality between the black and the white community self-sustaining output or maintainable consumer spending depends heavily upon the income class mobility of all sectors of the urban community. And since income class mobility is directly associated with the mobility rate of labor, which is associated directly with changes in the aggregate wage bill, the income class immobility in the black ghetto of the urban community holds down the aggregate wage bill in relation to total output and thereby reduces effective demand in the midst of poverty. This deficiency in effective demand in relation to total output *must either be made up out of social welfare payments to the black community from the white community,* or the black community must be allowed to own and organize the private capital resources in the black ghettos and make up the deficiency in the aggregate wage bill out of community receipts of profits, rent, interest, and dividends.

# Chapter 7

# A GHETTO
# INCOME-EXPENDITURE
# MODEL

If the black community faces an economic system that generates income inequality and relative poverty, it is clear that the black community as a whole cannot escape poverty. If, however, the black community could somehow receive profits as well as wages, it would be possible to counteract to some extent the conditions of income inequality and income class immobility among black workers. Receipt of profits by the black community is conceivable under conditions that include economic reorganization and restructuring of the black ghetto. Reallocation of resources within the ghetto could be based upon total expenditures within the ghetto and total receipts emanating from those expenditures in the form of wages, interest, profit, and dividends. This basis probably represents the only alternative open to the ghetto for combating the exogenous forces of income inequality generated by the rest of the economy. The central problem of the ghetto, therefore, is to organize a circuit flow of goods and money within the ghetto economy, raising effective demand of the ghetto community for the ghetto-produced goods and services it most urgently needs.

This interplay of ghetto buying and selling in a ghetto-controlled market economy may be illustrated in terms of a circular flow of incomes and expenditures among ghetto households and ghetto community-owned firms, as shown in Figure 7-1.

Ghetto households obtain money incomes by selling labor services to the ghetto community-owned firms and firms outside the ghetto. They use their money income to buy consumer goods and services from ghetto, community-owned firms. As shown in Figure 7-1, ghetto community-owned firms spend money to employ ghetto labor and capital resources in order to produce at a profit goods and services most wanted by ghetto consumers. Also, in the production of consumer goods, ghetto community-owned firms buy and sell to each other in order to put unemployed labor to work. Since community-owned firms represent community ownership of capital resources, all business surplus net of depreciation, taxes, and reserves are redistributed to the ghetto community in the form of interest, dividends, and profits.

The theory and the conditions of how this circuit flow of goods and money will work out in the black ghettos of central cities constitute the crux of black development. The economic end sought is black community receipts of the whole of the product of value added (wages, interest on capital, dividends, economic rent, and profits) from all stages of production (manufacturing through retail).

Private ownership of all businesses in the ghetto would be replaced by community ownership. These businesses would be community-owned in the sense that a public utility is municipally owned

Figure 7-1.  Circuit Flow of Commodities and Income

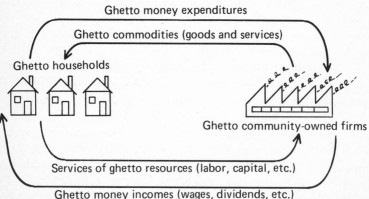

Ghetto money expenditures
Ghetto commodities (goods and services)
Ghetto households
Ghetto community-owned firms
Services of ghetto resources (labor, capital, etc.)
Ghetto money incomes (wages, dividends, etc.)

by the taxpayers. There would be a wide diversification of stock ownership among ghetto residents (only one vote regardless of number of shares owned) where the business unit is a corporation; all the stock in the community-owned corporation would be owned by resident stockholders. In the case where the business unit is a cooperative enterprise, all stock purchases would be limited to local ghetto residents. Thus, all corporate or cooperative profits, except retained earnings for depreciation and reinvestment, would go to the ghetto residents.

## NATIONAL GHETTO DEVELOPMENT CORPORATION

This reorganization, of course, would apply to all businesses located within the central city area where the population is 50 percent or more nonwhite. In this case the area would be declared by the federal government to be a black ghetto and affected with a public interest. The public utility concept would be extended to all business units within the area, including apartment buildings. Businesses would be operated only with a franchise from the federal government, and the franchise would be vested only in publicly-owned corporations. These firms would be part of the National Ghetto Development Corporation (NGDC) under the auspices of the federal government. NGDC would be empowered to purchase all ghetto businesses through condemnation proceedings and would operate them on behalf of the residents of the black community. The residents would be represented by a community-owned public corporation functioning as a holding company of all ghetto enterprises, to be known as (for example) National Ghetto Community Enterprises, Incorporated.

The National Ghetto Development Corporation would initiate throughout the United States the establishment of new and economically feasible enterprises (manufacturing, wholesale, and retail) that could maximize the income of ghetto residents. As these new enterprises become profitable they would be sold to National Ghetto Community Enterprises, Incorporated, at cost on a long-term payment basis. The purchase of existing businesses or the establishment of new businesses by the NGDC and subsequent sale of all such businesses to National Ghetto Community Enterprises would proceed according to a planned program of economic expansion of community ownership of capital resources by the black community. Capital expansion in the black community would proceed in accordance with a planned and systematic program geared to an annual target rate of capital growth among the various types of enterprises, particularly those showing the highest economic feasibility for all stages of production in terms of: (a) nature and scope of ghetto consumer demand; (b) income elasticity per dollar of capital investment; and (c) employment elasticity per dollar of capital investment.

This economic reorganization of ghetto resources, particularly the development of ghetto community-owned enterprises, is considered absolutely essential to a significant, organized program of development planning in the interest of the residents of the ghetto.

The basic plan is to restructure the ghetto so that employment outside the ghetto will generate, at each productive stage within the ghetto, along with vertical integration where feasible, the maximum rise in value added. The sum of value added at all stages will go to ghetto residents. Maximization of the size and industry mix of ghetto community output and allocation of the whole product to residents are essential to making up for the failure of market forces to move ghetto workers to higher income classes.

Figure 7-2 shows the financial reorganization and income reallocation of the ghetto in terms of a system of black monopoly. The proposed financial structure is designed to facilitate the assembling of large aggregations of liquid funds for both long-term and short-term production credit needs for ghetto development. Government treasuries, at the very top of Figure 7-2, represent the main source of initial subscription of capital stock for the establishment of a National Ghetto Development Corporation (NGDC), estimated to be about $40 billion. The NGDC would comprise a federal ghetto loan system consisting of National Ghetto Investment Banks for long-term credit and National Ghetto Credit Corporations for short-term production credit. These federal credit institutions would improve the credit standing of black community borrowers, who in this case would be ghetto community corporations, functioning as subsidiaries of National Ghetto Community Enterprises, Incorporated.

147

## Figure 7-2. Ghetto Financial Reorganization and Income Reallocation

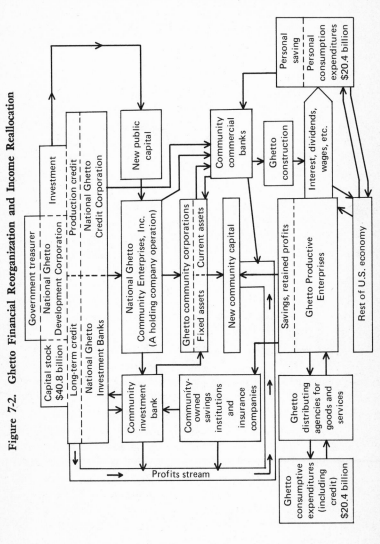

*Based upon a national Assets/Sales ratio of 2.06

## NATIONAL GHETTO INVESTMENT BANKS

A National Ghetto Investment Bank (NGIB) would be located in each of twelve major cities,[1] representing twelve districts, forming a reasonable cross-section of the national ghetto economy. The board of directors of each bank would include a representative from the NGDC.

The capital stock of each bank would be set at $1 billion, to be provided out of the initial capital subscription of $40 billion for NGDC. Although the $40 billion subscription would be open to private investors, any deficiencies in this required amount would be subscribed by the U.S. Treasury.

The NGIB would lend only to community investment banks, which would occupy a position analogous to the individual member banks of the Federal Reserve System. They would be in an intermediate position between the NGIB and the community borrowers —the ghetto community corporations. However, the community banks would differ in one most important respect from commercial banks in that they are community-owned banks organized by the community for the express purpose of securing long-term credit from NGIB.

The local community investment banks may, therefore, borrow from the National Ghetto Investment Banks only for purposes of meeting the fixed capital requirements of ghetto community-owned corporations. This is shown on the left side of Figure 7-2. Arrows indicate the flow of funds from the national bank to the community bank and then to ghetto community corporations. These borrowings may take the form of securities (notes and bonds) that flow upward through the community investment banks to the NGIB where they are ultimately lodged. The NGIB may in turn issue federal agency bonds to the general public as an additional source of funds.

The initial capital stock of each of these community investment banks would be set at $500 million, to be subscribed in part by local community residents in denominations of $5.00 per share. Any deficiencies in the subscribed amount would be subscribed by National Ghetto Community Enterprises, Inc., as the controlling corporate

---

[1] The twelve cities are Boston, New York City, Philadelphia, Washington (D.C.), Atlanta, New Orleans, Houston, St. Louis, Chicago, Detroit, Cleveland, and Los Angeles.

body of all ghetto enterprises operating within the ghetto economy. Funds for such purposes would come from stock subscriptions in the holding company, whose sale of stock would be nationwide in scope among ghetto residents. Also, it would be expected that additional potential sources of funds would come from private grants of agencies such as churches, and philanthropic institutions. All of these grant dollars would represent an investment that would generate a stream of income into the indefinite future.

## NATIONAL GHETTO CREDIT CORPORATIONS

On the right-hand side of Figure 7-2, the arrows show the flow of funds for working capital required of ghetto community-owned corporations. These funds flow downward from the National Ghetto Credit Corporation (NGCC), a federal institution, to community-owned commercial banks for short-term loans to community corporations. These short-term credit needs may be financed by the discount of promissory notes, accounts receivable, and the like, at community-owned commercial banks. Those banks, in turn, may borrow against this commercial paper at NGCC where these short-term securities are ultimately lodged.

Credit corporations would be located in each of the same twelve cities as NGIBs. The initial capital stock of each credit corporation would be set at $300 million, to be provided by NGDC. Loans would be made only to community-owned commercial banks, specifically for short-term production credit needs of ghetto community corporations, including ghetto residential construction.

In addition to community-owned investment and commercial banks, Figure 7-2 shows community-owned savings institutions (thrift institutions), savings and loans, pension funds, mutual savings, and community-owned insurance companies, to accumulate savings generated by new productive enterprises. All of these savings and insurance institutions help to avoid leakage of funds from the ghetto as well as serve as a main source of accumulating savings that are expected to flow from these institutions upward to community investment banks. Some savings may also flow directly to community-owned commercial banks. In any event, savings will be accumulated either through community investment banks, to finance fixed assets of the community-owned corporations, or through the community-owned commercial banks, to finance current assets of the community-owned corporations. As a result of these savings, new community capital will be generated.

The importance of ghetto community savings is shown in the lower part of Figure 7-2, where it is noted on the left that ghetto consumer expenditures, including credit buying and expenditure of welfare receipts, are estimated at $20.4 billion. Under present conditions, however, there are no savings (Chapter 3). Ghetto community ownership of all ghetto distributing agencies for goods and service, together with productive enterprises (manufacturing), would generate a rise in savings, as shown by ghetto income (Figure 7-2). Observe that $20.4 billion were spent on consumption with no savings (left side of figure). On the right, $20.4 billion were spent on consumption with savings for capital growth. The difference in savings is accounted for by the dotted lines with arrows that show the flow of interest, dividends, profits, and wages to ghetto households. Note that there is also an inflow of income (wages) from the rest of the U.S. economy.

It is clear that with more ghetto community control over the outflow of funds, *a black monopoly system will generate development and growth as long as the inflow of money from the rest of the U.S. economy is greater than outflow of money. That is, growth will depend upon the annual net inflow of funds that are saved and converted to new capital.*

A net inflow of dollars to the ghetto will represent a reversal of the present situation and help close the demand gap discussed in Chapter 3 (only a small fraction of total business receipts go to ghetto households). We note from Figure 7-2 that ghetto consumer expenditures represent a money flow to ghetto distributing agencies and productive enterprises (manufacturing units) with a return flow of goods and services to ghetto households.

The development and operation of this black monopoly system will depend heavily upon the National Ghetto Development Corporation. NGDC will not only initiate the development of new enterprises and bring them to a "going concern" level of performance before selling to the holding company, but will exercise a general coordinating function at the national level. National Ghetto Community Enterprises, Inc. will coordinate the needs of the local ghetto corporations to be established in various ghettos throughout the country.

All of the ghetto community corporations will come under the general management of National Ghetto Community Enterprises, Inc., which will function as a holding company of all of the ghetto community corporations. In addition to the general management function, National Ghetto Community Enterprises (with MDTA assistance) would conduct a ghetto manpower and training program designed to upgrade the skills and productivity of unskilled ghetto workers.

## MAXIMIZING GHETTO INCOMES

Assuming a black community-owned monopoly of capital resources, the concept of optimum economic relationship between the white and black community does not imply a condition of forced segregation among these communities. It is assumed, however, that for economic, political, and social reasons, the preponderance of the urban black population will tend increasingly to live in all-black communities in the central cities of the United States. Given the continued existence of black and white communities, however, optimum economic relationship with the white community means maximization of the share of the national income going to the black community residents (ghetto households) in the forms of interest, rent, dividends, and profits as well as wages and salaries. Maximization of the black community's share of national income could occur by maximization of the increase in the circuit flow of money and goods within the ghetto between the community households and community-owned business units, assuming no significant change in the level of employment discrimination. This implies that, for a given volume of ghetto household expenditures, there will be a rise in the proportion of the aggregate business receipts from these households going to nonwhite community-owned enterprises (closed community-owned corporations and cooperatives) together with a rise in the respending of business receipts within the ghetto for both capital imports from outside the ghetto and locally produced consumer goods. Thus, for a given annual rate of flow of aggregate ghetto household income from all sources, the ghetto's maximized share of the gross national product comprises the sum of that income plus the maximum proportion of income flow that can be diverted to community-owned corporations in the form of business receipts and respent in the form of factor payments during the year.

In these terms the aggregate annual income of ghetto residents could be increased by an acceleration of the rate of flow of money and goods (a rise in income velocity) between ghetto households and ghetto business units owned by ghetto households. This could be accomplished by accelerating the process of spending and re-spending of a given volume of dollars coming into and remaining in the ghetto community. Assuming no change in the rate of ghetto household spending, a net overflow of dollars would reduce the level of aggregate ghetto income.

Therefore, starting with a given rate of inflow of dollars per year into the ghetto community, aggregate household income in the ghetto community could be raised by converting these dollars into business receipts and returning these dollars (through investment) to ghetto households in the form of wages (from inside and out-side of the ghetto economy), together with dividends, interest, rent, and profits earned within the ghetto. Any rise in the inflow of dol-lars from outside the ghetto, would, of course, have a multiplier effect upon the generation of additional income within the ghetto, depending upon the rate of investment and respending within the ghetto, and assuming no leakage of dollars to outside sources.

## DEVELOPING A RATE OF GROWTH

If there were no net rise in the level of ghetto investment, the ag-gregate real income of ghetto households would at any given time remain static at constant prices and constant household spending rates. Assuming no leakage of income to the white community, a static condition in income flow within the ghetto would occur when gross investment in the ghetto is just sufficient to cover depreciation on the existing capital stock employed in the ghetto (that is, when gross investment minus depreciation equals zero).

Under static conditions the aggregate real income of the ghetto would remain constant, but the per capita real income of ghetto resi-dents would fall because of an increase in ghetto population (in-migration plus the natural rate of reproduction). So, in order to avoid a declining per capita real income in the ghetto, the volume of capital investment (gross investment in any one year) must not only be sufficient to cover depreciation on existing capital but must be enough so that the net growth of capital in the ghetto would exceed the net growth of the ghetto population.

Ghetto incomes are such that one may not expect any significant amount of personal savings, and therefore no net investment from personal savings. Therefore, a ghetto-owned economy would be doomed to a condition of falling per capita real income, if there were no additional inflow of income from outside the ghetto (rise in the level of the current inflow of wages, money capital, or even welfare payments).

A rise in the level of wage inflow to the ghetto could raise the circuit flow of goods and services to a higher aggregate level of real income. This could occur if an additional increment of capital could be borrowed from outside the ghetto economy (a rise in the import of capital goods from the white community) and be paid for out of additional wages earned outside the ghetto economy (a rise in the export of labor to the white community).

A constant annual rise in the aggregate level of real income in the ghetto would depend upon the annual increment to the aggregate wage bill of ghetto workers employed outside the ghetto, and, of course, the extent to which the net addition to the wage bill outside the ghetto economy is converted to ghetto capital (use of a rise in labor exports to pay for a rise in capital imports).

## A LABOR THEORY OF GROWTH

The production function of the labor-intensive ghetto is conceived of in terms of a labor theory of growth where the rise in the value product of the ghetto sector is a function of the capitalized value of the rise in earnings from employment outside the ghetto. This is in sharp contrast to a capital theory of growth where the rise in the value product is due directly to the capitalization of savings out of current income. That is, savings rise; and where saving equals investment, investment rises, and depending upon the capital/output ratio and the amount of savings, incomes rise, which leads to more savings, more investment, more income, and the like.[2] In this case, all surplus value (gross business surplus) is appropriated by the capitalist, assuming no rise in wages as productivity rises.

In terms of a labor theory of growth, all surplus value emanating from a rise in labor productivity would accrue to labor, provided labor could be swapped for capital, in which case, a given money value of labor would equal a given money value of capital. This could occur if labor exports from the ghetto could be swapped directly for capital imports from the capitalistic sector. Such a swap could occur if the addition to the total value of output in the ghetto (additional value added at all stages) could be purchased within the ghetto economy out of the factor payments occasioned by the additional value of output. Ordinarily, this would not be possible, since part of the value added (factor payments) includes the cost of capital that was produced outside the ghetto. However, the equivalent of the amount of capital cost deficiency in ghetto earnings and purchases could be made up out of additional earnings of ghetto residents employed outside the ghetto economy. Purchases in the ghetto from these additional earnings would complete the swap of ghetto labor for imported capital. In such a case, a rise in earnings of ghetto residents employed outside the ghetto could lead, when the new earnings are spent in the ghetto, to a rise in capital within the ghetto, and thereby to a rise in returns to labor employed in the ghetto at all stages. Since the source of capital within the ghetto would not originate out of savings within the ghetto, but out of the returns to redundant ghetto labor (labor with no alternative opportunity costs) employed outside the ghetto, the capital cost out of total value added within the ghetto is free to the ghetto economy as a whole. That is, there would be no social cost of capital to the ghetto economy. Therefore, labor (the ghetto community) would be entitled to the whole product (total of wages plus profits after paying the cost of imported capital from outside earnings).

So, starting with a given rate of inflow of dollars per year into the ghetto community from earnings in the capitalistic sector, aggregate household income in the ghetto community could be raised if an additional increment of capital could be borrowed from outside the ghetto community (a rise in the import of capital goods from the white community) and paid for from additional wages

[2] See Harrod-Domar Model. R. F. Harrod, *Towards a Dynamic Economics* (New York: St. Martin's Press, 1948).

earned outside the ghetto community (a rise in the export of unemployed labor to the white community). A rise in the export of unemployed labor to the white community would depend primarily upon the rate of capital expansion in service industries outside the ghetto community where black workers are over-represented. The rate of expansion in these service industries would, of course, depend upon the rate of rise in the national income.

Thus, if the aggregate wage bill of the economy as a whole rises annually by, say, 7.3 percent (going back to our earlier example), and the aggregate wage bill of ghetto workers due to increased employment of unemployed ghetto labor rises annually by 4.24 percent, the annual increment of wage-inflow going to previously unemployed ghetto residents would be 4.24 percent of the aggregate ghetto wage bill, the money value of which would represent the labor cost of the annual increment to capital.

Assuming an autonomous inflow of capital to the ghetto at the prevailing market rate of interest, the aggregate rate of rise in ghetto community real income would then depend upon: (1) the rate of capital expansion in low-paying service industries and occupations where black workers are predominantly employed outside the ghetto; (2) the annual increment to the wage bill of ghetto workers resulting from a rise in capital expansion in these service industries outside the ghetto; and (3) the extent to which the net addition to the aggregate wage bill of ghetto residents employed outside the ghetto is converted to capital (use of a rise in labor exports to pay for a rise in capital imports). In this case, the production function of the ghetto could be written as

$Y = (L_E, L_K, L_D)$, where
$Y =$ total ghetto output
$L_E =$ labor exported to white capital
$L_K =$ exported labor converted to black capital imports invested in the ghetto
$L_D =$ labor employed in the local black ghetto

In applying this production function to the ghetto economy, we assume the beginnings of three economic subsectors in the ghetto community: a *capital goods sector,* consisting of manufacturing operations based upon the import of machines, equipment, and raw material from outside the ghetto economy; a *consumer goods sector,* consisting of wholesale and retail operations generated by manufacturing in the capital goods sector; and a *labor export sector,* representing otherwise unemployed ghetto labor employed outside the ghetto community by white capital. The intersectoral flow of resources between these three sectors is illustrated in Table 7-1.

The following is observed:

1. The total output of the economy (GNP) was 7,000.
2. The capital goods sector (manufacturing operations) bought its machines and raw materials from outside of the black economy.
3. The value of imports of machines and raw materials (2,000) was paid for by the export of 2,000 worth of labor.
4. The capital goods sector is vertically integrated with the consumer goods sector (wholesale and retail operations).
5. The money value of the purchases for the wholesale opera-

Table 7-1.  Intersectoral Flow of Resources in a Three-Sector Labor-Intensive Ghetto Economy

|  | Capital goods sector | Consumer goods sector | | Labor export sector |  |
|---|---|---|---|---|---|
|  | Manu- facturing opera- tions | Whole- sale opera- tions | Retail opera- tions | Labor employed outside the black community | Value of output |
| Capital imports Borrowed capital |  |  |  |  |  |
| a) Machines | 1,000 |  |  |  | 1,000 |
| b) Raw material | 1,000 |  |  |  | 1,000 |
| c) Stock, merchandise |  | (3,000)* | (4,000)* |  |  |
| Wages | 700 | 700 | 700 | 2,000 | 4,100 |
| Profits | 300 | 300 | 300 |  | 900 |
| Value of out- put (Sales) | 3,000 | 1,000 | 1,000 | 2,000 | 7,000 |
| Payments for imports |  |  |  | (2,000) | −2,000 |
| Net value of output in the black community |  |  |  |  | 5,000 |

* Excluded to avoid double counting

tions in the consumer goods sector must equal the output of the manufacturing operations in the capital goods sector, and the purchases of the retail operations of the consumer goods sector must equal the output of the wholesale operations of the consumer goods sector.

6. There is no producer goods sector. All producer goods are imported and paid for out of earnings from otherwise unemployed labor exported to the white community.

7. The export sector is the balancing factor for general equilibrium. Since this ghetto economy does not produce its own machines and raw materials for manufacturing, it runs a deficit in its trade balance, and would have to cut back 2,000 on capital purchases or make up the deficit by exports that do not require machines for its production. Export of labor bringing in wages of 2,000 would wipe out the import deficit and the economy would be in equilibrium.

8. In terms of the ghetto production function, it is observed that

$$Y = L_E\,(2{,}000) + L_K\,(2{,}900) + L_D\,(2{,}100) = 7{,}000.$$

9. The total value added in the ghetto community (wages + profits) at all stages was 3,000.

10. The 2,000 earned outside the ghetto and converted to capital within the ghetto generated a net value of output of 5,000. Thus, the output/capital ratio $\frac{5{,}000}{2{,}000} = 2.5$, that is, \$1.00 of borrowed capital would yield \$2.50 in net value of output in this hypothetical model.

In Chapter 9, we shall apply this model to the Newark ghetto where the actual capital/output ratio is shown to depend upon the choice of technology (extent of labor-using capital in the ghetto), the type of manufacturing enterprises, and the size.

## The Rate of Employment and Output Within the Ghetto

Given the rate of capital expansion in these service industries where black workers are overrepresented outside the ghetto, the growth rate of the ghetto economy becomes a function of (1) the annual increment to the wage bill of ghetto residents employed outside the ghetto and (2) the net increase in local ghetto employment and output attributable to the conversion to capital of the annual increment to aggregate ghetto wage bill from outside the ghetto economy. The extent of this conversion of outside earnings to capital and the effects upon employment and output within the ghetto may be termed the incremental-labor-output ratio (ILOR).

If we let $V_g$ equal the total value added from all stages of ghetto production; and let the net increment to aggregate ghetto wage bill equal $L_E$, where $L_E$ equals $L_K$, the value of the conversion to capital of the net increment to the ghetto wage bill; then, $\dfrac{\Delta V_g}{V_g}$, the growth rate of ghetto output, equals the capital-import ratio, $\dfrac{L_K}{V_g}$, divided by the incremental-labor-output ratio, $\dfrac{L_K}{\Delta V_g}$

That is, $\dfrac{\Delta V_g}{V_g} = \dfrac{\dfrac{L_K}{V_g}}{\dfrac{L_K}{\Delta V_g}}.$

Therefore $G$, the ghetto economy growth rate, equals the labor export ratio divided by the incremental labor output ratio, or $\dfrac{L_E}{L_K}$. And where $L_E = L_K$, labor is entitled to that portion of value added that would normally go to capital as net income.

Assuming the incremental-labor-output ratio is to remain fixed, the rate of capital expansion, employment, and output in the ghetto could be increased only by a rise in the rate of export of ghetto labor to the capitalistic sector. But the trend of technology in manufacturing industries is such that the annual rate of rise in ghetto labor exports will depend primarily upon the rate of capital expansion in constant returns service industries with fixed labor/capital ratios.

Given the annual rate of rise in ghetto labor exports, however, with a fixed ILOR, the equivalent rate of expansion in ghetto capital imports (that is, $L_E = L_K$) would raise the aggregate level of spending (payments and receipts within the ghetto) by an amount indicated by the net output/capital ratio. That is, recalling our input/output table, if $1.00 in borrowed capital yields $2.50 in net value added, $2,000 in additional labor exports converted to capital would add $5,000 in wages and profits to the circuit flow of money and goods in the ghetto. Since we assume no personal savings in the ghetto, that is, the annual cost of capital (annual depreciation) is paid for out of otherwise unemployed labor exports, we may say that the multiplier effect of the additional capital investment would equal 1. This, of course, assumes no leakage of dollars to the capitalistic sector.

This rise in aggregate wages and profits generated by a rise in unemployed labor exports would accelerate the annual rate of flow of goods in the ghetto by the spending and respending of a larger volume of dollars, and thereby raise the level of the circuit flow of money and goods. Thus, for any given year, the total net addition to income of the ghetto community would consist of: (a) the total value of output generated by new capital (including the cost of capital, plus the additional wages and profits earned within the economy, plus the additional earning from labor exports) minus the cost of total capital imports, including capital replacement; and (b) the net value of (a) above multiplied by the income velocity in the ghetto.

## The Growth Path of the Ghetto Economy

As long as there were a continuous net rise in the export of otherwise unemployed ghetto labor whose earnings are continuously converted to capital, the growth path of the ghetto economy would represent a moving equilibrium through time as long as $L_E = L_K$. This growth path would continue until the redundant supply of ghetto labor was fully employed, at which time, the marginal value productivity and wage of ghetto labor employed outside the ghetto in low-paying service industries would tend to rise to the level of the higher marginal value productivity and wage of ghetto workers employed in ghetto manufacturing operations.

This process of ghetto economy growth is graphically illustrated in Figures 7-3a and 7-3b.

In Figure 7-3a, $OL$ represents the total supply of ghetto labor, of which $L_0L$ is unemployed. In Figure 7-3a, $L_0L$ equals $OL'$ in

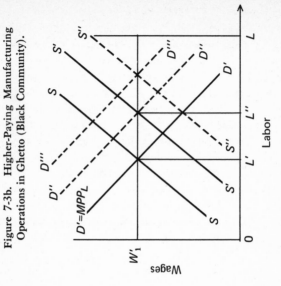

Figure 7-3b. Higher-Paying Manufacturing Operations in Ghetto (Black Community).

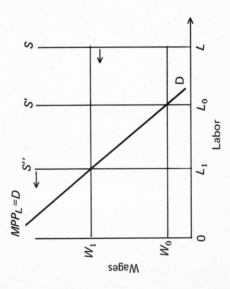

Figure 7-3a. Lower-Paying Service Sector Outside the Ghetto (White Community).

Figure 7-3b. Figure 7-3a shows that in the lower-paying service sector outside the ghetto, the marginal physical productivity of labor (curve $DD$) is such that the wage falls to $W_0$ (the legal minimum), and that at this low wage the supply of labor in the ghetto for the service sector in the white community is unlimited. Only $OL_0$ amount will be employed at $W_0$ wage rate, however, and $L_0L$ amount of labor will remain unemployed out of the total available supply at point $L$.

Figure 7-3b applies to an emerging manufacturing operation in the labor-intensive ghetto sector. The ghetto manufacturing operations are in competition with the rest of the economy and have employed more capital. Hence, the marginal productivity of labor is higher in the ghetto manufacturing operation than in the lower-paying service sector where the capital-labor ratio is low.

The higher productivity of manufacturing operations is shown by the wage rate, $W_1$ where $OW_1'$ is greater than $OW_0$.

Because of the difference in wage rates, ghetto workers will want to move into ghetto manufacturing operations, but they cannot because of the shortage of capital. If some portion of the pool of ghetto unemployed could swap their labor in the white community for capital to be employed in ghetto manufacturing operations, the $D'D'$ curve or demand for labor shifts to the right $D''$ as shown in Figure 7-3b. Assuming no change in technology, that is, no rise in capital intensity, more labor will be employed. A rise in capital intensity is unlikely, however, because of the volume of unemployed labor. Additional unemployed labor could be employed at a constant wage rate until a time when all surplus labor is absorbed by the ghetto and nonghetto labor market. When all surplus labor is employed, the expanding ghetto manufacturing operations will continuously employ more labor by attracting workers from the service sector of the white community until the wage rates are equal in both the black and white community. This is shown in Figures 7-3a and 7-3b where $OW_1' = OW_1$.

# Chapter 8

# ECONOMIC DEVELOPMENT: PROBLEMS AND THEORY

## WHAT TO PRODUCE

If we view the ghetto as a labor-intensive economy separate from the white community, which is capital intensive, how can the black community decide how to utilize its growing supply of black labor? If the problems of economic separateness and income inequality did not exist, the best use of the labor would be to export black labor to the white community. There it would be combined with high-productivity capital to yield a higher productivity of labor. The proceeds of this employment could then be used to meet the economic demand of the ghetto. The ghetto community would bid for produced resources (goods) on equal terms with the affluent white community, which bids for the labor resources it needs. Abundant high-productivity labor would be exchanged for abundant goods and services. Serious income inequality does exist, however, since the question of what to produce in the economy is determined mainly by the higher-income segment of the white community, the black community is left with the open question of what it should produce with its own underemployed and unemployed labor.

The impact of the demand of middle- and higher-income white consumers diverts resources away from the basic economic needs of the black community. A good example of this is the construction industry, which has concentrated its new construction in the more affluent white community. Little or no new private construction takes place in the black community. Higher incomes in the white community and higher prices have performed their rationing functions of depriving the black community of its more urgent need—adequate housing. Thus, black labor employed outside the ghetto may end up assisting in the production of goods designed and produced to meet the higher demand of the white community via a price system that prices poor people out of the market in the area of basic social needs such as housing and education.

## DIVERSION OF LABOR RESOURCES

In the white capitalistic sector, almost universally, occupation by occupation, industry by industry, workers from the black community experience a higher incidence of low earnings than white workers. Therefore, another basic problem all black communities face is how to prevent the continuous diversion of productive labor resources away from their community. The present system of resource allocation results in serious inequalities in wage income between black and white workers. Stated another way, the basic problem of all black communities is how to exercise more control in developing more productive utilization of labor in the black and white communities. This means determining, within the constraints of serious income inequality between the black and white community, how productive processes in the black community can be organized to raise the productivity of black labor in meeting the basic economic and social needs of the black community. The solution to this problem obviously points to some basic changes in the economic organization and industry mix of the black community.

## COMBINING BLACK LABOR WITH WHITE CAPITAL

Perhaps the most fundamental problem is how black labor resources are to be combined with white capital both within and outside the black ghetto. The general case is one where black labor is combined with white capital mostly at low levels of pay. That is, the demand for black labor is generally a demand for cheap labor to be employed in low-productivity jobs and industries. The evidence for this is that the proportion of full-time black workers earning poverty wages (under $3,000) is three to five times the proportion of white workers in the same jobs and industries. This is shown in Table 3, Chapter 2. Observe that in the construction industry, in manufacturing, and in trade, the proportion of black workers receiving poverty wages was over five times the proportion of white workers.

Now, it ·is undoubtedly profitable for the individual white capitalist to hire cheap black labor for low-productivity jobs. But this condition of profitability in the white community in the use of black labor is at the expense of the black community. This is because the black community has only labor to sell, and when its labor is sold at a low price this affects the terms of trade between cheap black labor from the ghetto community and oligopoly-priced consumer goods from the white community. The economic results constitute a permanent condition of poverty in the black community, unless the profits arising from the use of cheap black labor could be made to accrue to the black community as a whole. The black community as a whole could receive the profits from cheap black labor by the expansion of labor-using black-owned capital and technology in its own community. In a labor-intensive economy with unemployed labor, such as the black ghetto, economy in the use of labor resources would dictate those types of enterprises involving a high ratio of labor to capital. The principle involved is to economize on the scarce factor, capital, while making free use of the plentiful factor, labor. The policy implications of this principle of economy of factoral combination in the black ghetto is that the main thrust of ghetto development should be in the direction of labor-using enterprises. The economic objectives of labor-using enterprises in the ghetto would be a reversal of technological objectives sought in the capitalistic sector of the economy where unskilled black labor, as already shown, is becoming redundant to technological processes.

# THE EFFECTS OF TECHNOLOGICAL UNEMPLOYMENT

Perhaps the most pernicious problem faced by the black community is the economic effects of rapid technological change upon the demand for unskilled black labor in high-productivity manufacturing industries. Technological change, which reallocates black labor to low-paying jobs in trade and service industries, is undoubtedly a major contributory factor to the depression rates of ghetto unemployment, even during periods of prosperity. For example, during the first nine months of 1969, 8.0 percent of all black workers were unemployed. The incidence of this unemployment in the black community falls most heavily upon the new supply of black workers coming on the market annually. For example, the Bureau of Labor Statistics reports that one-fifth of out-of-school black teenagers are unemployed.[1]

Employment data show that for the economy as a whole an absolute reduction of unemployment rates to zero levels is not economically feasible, except perhaps under extreme and unacceptable conditions of inflation. In the case of the black community, it is more significant to note that the degree of unemployment associated with "full employment" under reasonable conditions of inflation leaves entirely unacceptable conditions of unemployment within the black community, yet employment rates in the black community continue to run at a two to one ratio between nonwhite and white. As previously pointed out, the economic effects of this chronic condition of unacceptable unemployment rates in the black community exert continuous downward pressure upon wage rates offered black workers. In terms of the supply of and the demand for black labor, we have a unique situation involving an infinitely elastic supply schedule of black workers at low wage rates. On the demand side, the black worker is confronted with a high degree of income inelasticity of demand for his services. This means that under conditions of technological change, the supply of black workers will always exceed the demand for black workers as the national income rises. Under such conditions, there will always

[1] U.S. Department of Labor, Bureau of Labor Statistics, *Social and Economic Conditions of Negroes in the United States,* Report No. 332 (Washington, D.C.: U.S. Government Printing Office), p. 34.

be a tendency for the supply curve of black labor to intersect the demand curve for black labor at the lowest possible wage level.

A substantial expansion of employment opportunities within a black-owned system could be made to counteract the effects of technological change on unemployment and low wage rates among ghetto residents. Assuming a black-owned system, ghetto residents would be confronted with two labor markets: the labor market within the system, and the labor market outside. These two labor markets for unskilled black labor (see Figure 8-1) would be characterized by wage differentials amounting to at least the cost of transportation for workers working outside the black community.

This market wage differential between $\dfrac{w}{P_0}$ and $\dfrac{w}{P_1}$ in Figure 8-1 is designated as $T$.

Assuming perfect mobility of black labor between these two labor markets, the following would occur:

1. Technological changes outside the ghetto would cause the demand curve for unskilled black labor outside the ghetto to shift downward to the (right) from $DD$ to $D'D'$ in Figure 8-1. The

**Figure 8-1. Two Markets for Ghetto Labor**

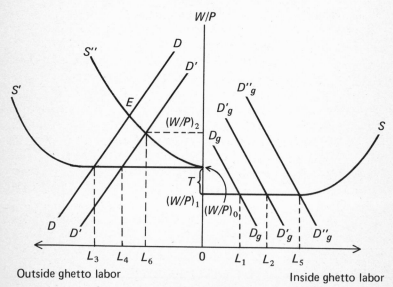

quantity of black labor demanded would fall from $L_3$ to $L_4$ with no change in wage rates.

2. In Figure 8-1, however, the demand for black labor inside the ghetto would shift upward to the right from $D_gD_g$ to $D_g'D_g'$, thereby increasing the quantity of labor employed from $L_1$ to $L_2$. This increase in employment in the ghetto system would tend to off-set the downward shift in the demand curve for labor outside and absorb some of the already existing unemployed labor.

3. Further upward shifts in the demand curve for labor in the ghetto system, as represented by $D_g''D_g''$ would exhaust all un-employed black labor, thereby reducing the quantity of labor in Figure 8-1 to $L_6$; for which quantity the short-run price for black labor is at $\dfrac{W}{P_2}$.

4. With all unemployed black labor exhausted, the supply curve for black labor outside the ghetto shifts upward to the left as shown by $S''$ and intersects the demand curve $D'D'$ at the higher equilibrium wage (point $E$).

## GENERATING CAPITAL GROWTH

If aggregate spending in the economy as a whole has very little allocational and efficiency effect upon living levels in the ghetto, the central problem facing the black ghetto is how spending in the ghetto can generate capital growth within the ghetto and change the present pattern of resource allocation. In 1969 I estimated that aggregate Negro expenditures (including excess of spending over receipts) was $34.5 billion. At least two-thirds of this aggregate Negro purchasing power goes for wages and salaries in the economy as a whole, and has a multiplier effect upon additional spending in the economy. But because of the Negro pattern of employment and wages, the Negro community does not share proportionately in the factor payments generated by his own expenditures, including his spending of receipts from welfare. Even profits on sales in the black community go mainly to the white community. Employment generated by Negro expenditures goes mainly to white workers. By the nature of the case, even the welfare payments to Negroes keep white workers employed at higher wages than Negroes. Ironically, ghetto spending of welfare checks generates receipt of wages, profits, rents, interests, and dividends in the white community, in return for which the ghetto residents receive subsistence welfare checks. In this respect, the bigger the welfare payments to ghetto residents, the greater the receipts of factor payments going to the white community. Of course, if the welfare recipients had jobs, the total output would be larger, but ghetto residents would not share proportionately in the factor receipts generated by their spending.

Finally, another central problem of development faced by the black ghetto is the problem of planned capital growth within the ghetto under conditions where the black community: (a) determines the priority and economic feasibility of what to produce in the black ghetto; (b) determines how to combine its unemployed labor resources with borrowed capital so as to optimize employment and wage income within the black community; and (c) determines its system of resource ownership and control so as to optimize the receipts of wages, interest, profits, rents, and dividends going to the black community as a whole. A program of planned capital expansion under the foregoing conditions would generate a rise in total output in the black community where factor payments would take the form of interest, profits, rents, and dividends, in addition to wages, and would tend to offset the growing reduction in the relative share of the per capita real income going to the black community.

## A BLACK-OWNED SYSTEM OF RESOURCE CONTROL

Our analysis of the central development problems faced by every black community assumes the development of a black-controlled system of ghetto development that would necessarily involve a high degree of autonomy in determining the allocation and utilization of resources within the black ghetto. The emphasis would be upon the basic problems involved in developing a more economical organization of capital and labor resources within the black community, to the end of raising the per capita real income of Negroes.

The specific problems involved in meeting these ends are considered problems endogenous to a black-owned system of resource control. The general problems endogenous to a black-owned system involve the poverty and economic impotence of the black community in a system of wealth and economic power. The traditional socially proscribed role of the Negro is no longer tenable and the general market solution is hardly applicable to the present situation. Market forces appear to be ineffective in the allocation of resources to an identifiable group of people occupying a delineated area in an urban community—people who are especially poor relative to the rest of the community and whose economic role has been socially proscribed. The problems endogenous to the development of such a community becomes a special case calling for a unique solution within the general structure of a mixed capitalistic system. No unique solution is possible, however, without some major concessions from the white power system. The basic problems of resource allocation in the black ghettos are generated by the system as a whole.

## THEORY OF BLACK COMMUNITY OWNERSHIP: BASIC ASSUMPTIONS

### Black Community Market Control in a System of Restricted Competition

In terms of economic power, the most relevant form of market organization in America is oligopoly—a system in which a few big firms dominate the market in each industry. The extent in this market concentration and control is seen in Table 8-1. Black monopoly theory, therefore, takes its cue from industrial concentration and control. Instead of concentration and control by industry, our theory of concentration and control is applied to a market area economy known as the black ghetto. While the concept of market area control is not new to American industry in terms of the geographic division of markets among a few big firms; control of a market area economy by the community is indeed a new concept. It is a concept that envisages the social economics of cost reduction among

Table 8-1.  Percent of Shipments Accounted for by Large
Manufacturing Companies, Selected Industries, 1963

| Industry | Percent shipped by four largest companies |
|---|---|
| Cigarettes | 80% |
| Motor vehicles and parts | 79 |
| Metal cans | 74 |
| Aircraft engines and parts | 72 |
| Tires and inner tubes | 70 |
| Aluminum rolling and drawing | 68 |
| Blast furnaces and steel mills | 69 |
| Petroleum refining | 34 |
| Meat slaughtering plants | 31 |
| Radio, TV communications equipment | 29 |
| Fluid milk | 23 |
| Aircraft | 59 |
| Bread and related products | 23 |
| Newspapers | 15 |
| Prepared animal feeds | 22 |
| Paper mills, except building | 26 |
| Pharmaceutical preparations | 22 |
| Sawmills and planing mills | 11 |
| Farm machinery and equipment | 43 |
| Canned fruits and vegetables | 24 |
| Construction machinery | 42 |
| Metal stampings | 13 |
| Printing, except lithographic | 13 |
| Plastics materials and resins | 35 |
| Paints and allied products | 23 |
| Dresses | 6 |
| Paperboard mills | 27 |
| Toilet preparations | 38 |

Source: U.S. Dept. of Commerce, Bureau of the Census, Concentration Ratios in
Manufacturing Industry (Washington, D.C.: U.S. Government Printing Office, 1963)
and unpublished data.

a large number of small high-cost uneconomic business units. This
is in sharp contrast to area market control by a few big firms whose
primary objective is to maximize profits, rather than a reduction in
the social cost of providing goods and services to a community.
Thus the underlying theory of a black power system of resource

control is a theory of market power used in the social interest instead of market power used to promote private interest.

## Derivation of the Concept of Black Community Monopoly

Black community monopoly, as a social instrument of market control, is grounded on a theory of social cost and stems from the fact that the black community pays more than the white community for goods and services.[2] The theory of social cost is derived from the concept of perfect competition, in which the long-run tendency of price would be to equal marginal cost. But since this long-run tendency of costs and prices does not prevail in ghetto markets, it is socially necessary to reduce the real cost of living in the ghetto by transferring profits to the black community as a whole. These profits represent the difference between social-cost pricing and the prices set on some other basis. This cost-of-living reduction could be achieved by restructuring the ghetto economy to reduce cost as much as possible and to transfering profits, interest, rents, and dividends to ghetto residents. Community monopoly control for this purpose would consist of a community-owned holding company operation controlling and developing all businesses operating in an area designated as a black ghetto. Such a holding company operation would start with a ready market within the ghetto consisting of $12–20 billion (total Negro purchasing power was $36.4 billion in 1969). On the basis of community monopoly control of such a mammoth market, economies of scale would become immediately feasible among all of the various types of enterprises that now operate in the ghetto under high cost conditions. In addition, the community-controlled holding company could develop many new types of enterprises, particularly certain types of manufacturing operations that would be vertically integrated with wholesale and retail operations. The total value added at the manufacturing, wholesale, and retail stages would then accrue entirely to the black ghetto in the form of wages, interest, profits, rents, and dividends.

[2] This refers to the terms of trade between black labor and oligopolistically priced goods. The prices paid by black labor for industrial goods become increasingly disproportionate to the prices received for black ghetto labor.

## Application of the Concept of Countervailing Power

Countervailing power, as applied by Galbraith,[3] points to the economic need of weaker economic groups to organize in order to countervail the power of stronger economic groups. For example, this implies the economic necessity of powerful unions to countervail the power of big business, or of both agricultural and consumer groups to exercise countervailing power against corporate establishments. If there is an economic need for countervailing power among labor groups, agricultural groups, and consumer groups, the case for countervailing power for the black group in the ghetto becomes overwhelming, particularly since that group derives little or no benefit from the economic power of other groups. Thus, the case for countervailing power among the black group must transcend functional distinctions, such as the labor group, the farm group, the consumer group, and so forth, and must apply to a poverty-stricken, racially, socially, and geographically segregated group representing an across-the-board economic weakness as laborer, farmer and consumer.

Under this unique set of economic conditions, the concept of countervailing power as applied to an area becomes the most economical way of meeting the needs of a poverty-stricken area as a whole. In this case, the concept implies a powerful area economic organization capable of countervailing the impact of economic forces emanating from the rest of the economy. A large community-owned holding company monopoly in the black area controlling a market of between $12 billion and $20 billion within the area could exercise a powerful bargaining force in the exchange of resources between the black ghetto and the rest of the economy.

## BLACK COMMUNITY OWNERSHIP THEORY APPLIED TO GHETTO DEVELOPMENT

The applicability of black community ownership theory in the American system of free enterprise is based primarily upon the sim-

[3] J. K. Galbraith, *American Capitalism: The Concept of Countervailing Power*, Revised ed. (Boston: Houghton Mifflin, 1956).

ple fact that income differentials between the black ghetto and the more affluent white community are not self-correcting through the price system. These income differentials rise primarily from differences in resource ownership consisting of differences in the quality of labor power owned, and differences in the nature and quantities of capital owned. These differences in resource ownership have become institutionalized over time because black people as a group have had no opportunity to improve the quality of their labor resources by acquiring specific types of training and no opportunity to accumulate capital either through savings or inheritance.

When the black man in America was released from slavery, he was an uneducated propertyless wage earner whose economic role was socially proscribed in an economy soon to become characterized by big business. Since then, the growth of industrial concentration has generated economic forces that have not only precluded the propertyless ex-slave from becoming a competing capitalist but have also created a new class of white propertyless wage earners who, through their trade union organizations, have kept the black masses of labor from competing for the better jobs.

We may say then that the black community represents a special case in the economic processes of the economy as a whole. When the black community is viewed as a separate economic entity, distinct differences can be seen in the pattern of employment, consumption, and income, and the rate of growth of these variables compared with the growth rate of output of the economy as a whole. Both impersonal economic forces, as well as the forces of social proscription, have generated a system of resource allocation and utilization that creates differentials in resource ownership among black and white people.

With respect to the future of the economic well-being of the black community, it appears that a rise in output in the capitalistic sector under conditions of technological change and oligopolistic pricing reduces the demand for black labor in the better-paying jobs, and over time reduces the relative share of the aggregate real wages going to the black community. As previously pointed out, the effects of this in the black community are equivalent to an increase in capital per laborer in the absence of technical change. The result is that output allocated in the black community does not increase proportionately to the increase in capital in the economy, thereby causing over time a relative decline in the per capita income of the black ghetto. A black-owned system of resource control becomes relevant and applicable to the extent that such a system can generate induced capital growth in the black community. In Chapter 9 we will analyze the possibility of induced capital growth in the ghetto under a black-owned power system based upon the exchange of black labor for white capital. Our theory of the conversion of black ghetto labor resources to capital resources is designed to show how a system of black-owned control of resources will generate a rise in total output in the black community, taking the form of interest, profits, rent, and dividends in addition to wages, and how the black-owned system would tend to offset the growing reduction in the relative share of the total output going to the black community.

## SUMMARY

In summary, we may say that the economic activities of the black ghetto communities throughout the United States have been expelled by the price system from the allocative processes of the economy as a whole. The backwash effect has resulted in an inefficient form of economic organization within the ghetto based upon an enclave of socially uneconomic business units with high cost and high prices selling to poor people, and in which no amount of rise in black consumer spending in the ghetto generates a rise in the aggregate received income of the ghetto. Any rise in ghetto consumer spending only serves to put the factors of production to work outside the ghetto. Increased production, because of the nature of production organization, generates no corresponding rise in the aggregate demand for unskilled ghetto labor. High rates of unemployment and underemployment persist in the ghetto despite high levels of output in the rest of the economy.

Therefore, the economic development of the black community will depend heavily upon gearing black community consumer spending to a system of ghetto resource organization that will have a generative effect upon the incomes of members of the ghetto community. This implies a system in which a rise in ghetto consumer spending will generate a rise in demand for ghetto community-owned resources (factors of production), whose receipts (factor payments) would constitute the aggregate cost (including capital cost) and the aggregate demand for the additional goods, and whose profits would be shared by residents of the ghetto community.

# Chapter 9

# ECONOMIC IMPLICATIONS OF BLACK COMMUNITY CONTROL

The economic implications of a black community system of resource control primarily involve supply and demand aspects. On the supply side, relevant theories of production, costs, pricing, output, and product distribution or factor payments are the main concerns. On the demand side, the system implies a unique pattern of black consumer demand under conditions of market area monopoly—those spatial and demand factors that differentiate both the product purchased and the nature of the demand schedule faced by the monopolist producer in the black community.

The term "monopoly" is not used here in its pure sense to mean there are no existing substitutes for ghetto-produced goods; we will discuss the possible but limited substitutability for ghetto-produced goods. We will also point out the derivation of monopolistic elements of spatial and racial factors from residential segregation; we will show how these elements affect the nature of black consumer decisions. For the purposes of our analysis, however, we will accept the assumptions of pure monopoly that are applicable to the concept of a black community monopoly.

Our concept is that for any given black ghetto community, a single national ghetto community-owned holding company corporation is the monopolist that would have the controlling interest in all enterprises operating in the ghetto area. This holding company would be able to act in a monopolistic fashion because entry of independent producers into the ghetto market area would be blocked. Further, the ghetto community-owned corporation would be the sole seller of consumer goods and services within the ghetto area. Any actions taken by the corporation within the ghetto area will not evoke retaliation by producers outside the ghetto and vice versa. The concept of monopoly is applicable, therefore, because the ghetto firm is a single, community-owned, independent, monopoly seller, whose aims are to expand employment and production, to lower production costs, to determine the level of output, and to increase income distribution through ghetto factor payments.

A black-owned system of resource control implies that a community-owned monopolist will determine within reasonable limits of economic feasibility what is to be produced within the black community, how the production is to be organized, how the products produced in the black community are to be distributed among its members, and how the productive capacity of the black community can be maximized, maintained, and expanded. Our first considerations will be those of supply and demand, and how to determine what to produce.

## GHETTO MARKET SUPPLY

If we accept the proposition that black ghettos are primarily one-sector labor-export economies, the determination of what to produce in the ghetto economy involves (1) determining the priority of wants of ghetto consumers as shown by their pattern of consumption and (2) determining, within the pattern of wants, the economic feasibility of import-substitute enterprises that would have the maximum effects upon employment of unemployed labor within the ghetto. The problem of the monopolist will be the coordination of ghetto demand with feasible labor-using enterprises within the ghetto.

### The Problem of Leakage

*Sources.* Leakage arises when factor payments (wages and profits) earned in the ghetto are used outside the ghetto. These leaked ghetto receipts from ghetto production of import substitutes may take the form of: (1) direct purchase of goods and services outside the ghetto; (2) savings and investment in outside financial institutions; or (3) purchases of "imported" goods and services within the ghetto.

Earnings of dollars brought back to the ghetto from the capitalistic sector may immediately leave the ghetto through purchases by consumers of imports. The idea of ghetto development and growth, however, presupposes either no leakage of dollars at all, or leakage that is less than the inflow of dollars to the economy. Our solution to the leakage problem involves optimizing the net inflow of dollars to the ghetto and closing the ghetto economic system to all transactions that do not contribute to the growth of the ghetto economy as a whole. Such transactions consist of (1) import of consumer goods and services (which could be internally produced) from the capitalistic sector for sale in the ghetto, and (2) purchase of goods and services outside the ghetto when similar goods and services are produced within the ghetto.

*Effects.* These transactions generate employment and income in the capitalistic sector at the expense of unemployed labor in the ghetto economy. Expansion in capital investment in the ghetto for retail sales of externally produced goods benefits external factors of production, the individual capitalist (black or white) within the ghetto, and a few workers. It does not raise the level of the circuit flow of goods and services in the ghetto due to leakage. Reduction of leakage involves: (1) monopolization of profits on consumer imports at the retail stage; (2) vertical integration, where feasible, of all stages of production in the ghetto (manufacturing, wholesaling, and retailing); and (3) local consumption of ghetto-produced goods. In this way, the ghetto economy maximizes its receipts of the total value added at all stages and sets up a continuous circuit flow of expenditures and receipts by an amount equal to total value added, net of leakage by the particular productive operations.

*Prevention.* The monopolist will be confronted with a current aggregate ghetto-earned income of $12 billion. All of this earned income could be spent in the ghetto area. If we add the amount of credit purchases and welfare receipts that we estimate to be about

$8 billion, this represents about a 70 percent increase in purchases over and above current earnings.[1]

If we followed the stringent assumption of pure monopoly, our system of black monopoly would be entirely closed to the leakage of all expenditures outside the ghetto. With these projected expenditures, however, a considerable amount of leakage could be tolerated without jeopardizing the circuit flow of money and goods generated by ghetto production. Nevertheless, since the system is not closed to all leakage, the objective is to maximize the net inflow of dollars. What type of industry mix would minimize leakage? The answer to this question is complicated by the fact that whatever industry mix is established, there will already be a similar industry mix outside the ghetto, and on a more intensive scale. Whatever is being produced in the ghetto will always be available outside the ghetto either for direct or indirect sale to ghetto residents. So the producer must study the current pattern of demand and supply. He will decide that the primary ghetto market for manufactured goods consists of goods now in demand that can be supplied by ghetto production factors. The goods and services the ghetto now imports from the capitalistic sector would be supplied the primary ghetto market economy at the wholesale and retail stage. The import of products for which ghetto manufacturing is not feasible would merely represent a market extension of the capitalistic sector at the manufacturing stage. The profits from distribution at wholesale and retail would, of course, go to the black community as dividends in a black monopoly system.

The problem of leakage is then reduced to those ghetto transactions that prohibit a return of factor payments as business receipts to ghetto producers. This type of leakage would occur if earnings from ghetto production were used to purchase goods directly or indirectly from the capitalistic sector; for example, if workers in a ghetto-owned shirt or furniture factory did not purchase the products of the factory. In the aggregate, leakage would occur if the equivalent of the total earnings of ghetto workers in the production of shirts, furniture, and so forth was not used to buy the total output of shirts, furniture, and so forth. In terms of our

[1] Based on Newark data. See Footnote 4, Chapter 3.

framework, however, this type of leakage is not likely. Earnings of ghetto residents who work inside and outside the ghetto would be used to purchase products, such as shirts and furniture, produced in the ghetto community-owned enterprises. In other words, the leakage problem would be resolved if the demand for ghetto-produced consumer goods was such that a given output of ghetto-produced goods would be purchased by ghetto consumers instead of imports they now purchase.

## Monopolization of Profits on Imports

Under a system of black community monopoly, the black community would receive profits from two sources: (1) import substitutes produced and purchased in the ghetto, and (2) imported consumer goods for which there is no import substitute. Under the present economic structure of the ghetto, the uncontrollable problem of leakage results from direct leakage of profits earned by white-owned businesses in the ghetto.[2] Owners employ their profits almost entirely outside the ghetto. Black monopoly under community ownership would eliminate this direct leakage. All profits of the community-owned corporation derived from the sale of consumer imports would be paid to the black community residents in the form of dividends.[3] These dividends, when added to ghetto resident wage receipts (earned both within and outside the ghetto) would represent ghetto resident personal income before taxes. Thus, the profits formerly leaked would be converted, through black community ownership, to additional consumer purchasing power. (Profits on import substitutes would also be converted to consumer purchasing power although the leakage here is not caused by white ownership, but by competition between imported consumer goods and ghetto-produced import substitutes.)

The basic question is whether the supply costs of ghetto-produced import substitutes, including profits, will equal the business receipts for these goods. The supply costs are all business expendi-

---

[2] In the Newark ghetto, this amounted to $55.8 million out of an average of $215.7 million in gross sales, 1965–69 (see Chapter 3).

[3] Factor payments of $55.8 million would yield an average of $2,195 per family in Newark ghetto.

tures including the cost of capital. If part of these costs are used by the community to buy imported consumer goods, leakage will result in the circuit flow of money and ghetto-produced goods and services. This leakage of money from the ghetto production system would not be a leakage to the ghetto economy as a whole, since the economy is a community monopoly; nevertheless, this kind of leakage could divert ghetto resources away from development of import substitute industries.

*Keeping Ghetto Wage Receipts in the Ghetto.*  Under a system of black community monopoly, aggregate disposable income in the ghetto would consist of: (1) dividends from the community-owned corporation; (2) additional wage receipts earned in the ghetto generated by a rise in internal capital expansion and employment; and (3) total wages earned outside the ghetto. Under our theory of ghetto capital growth, wages earned outside the ghetto would be used to pay for ghetto capital imports (see Chapter 7). This theory of the swap of black labor for white capital assumes that the supply costs or factor payments from ghetto production of goods and services (import substitutes) will be returned as ghetto business receipts, including the cost of capital depreciation. This means that the leakage problem of ghetto wage receipts is confined to the supply costs of ghetto output covering all stages of production, including manufacturing. The leakage of wages does not apply to the wage portion of the supply costs of ghetto-imported consumer goods. By the time imported consumer goods reach the final retail stage in the ghetto, the bulk of the wage costs will have been paid.

*Consumer Purchase Dividends.*  The leakage of wage receipts from ghetto production may be avoided entirely if the monopoly corporation pays dividends on residents' purchases of ghetto-produced items. Dividends could be in the form of credit on stock purchases in the ghetto monopoly corporation, or cash payments at the end of the fiscal year. Payment would be based on purchasers' sales receipts at the end of the year. Dividends would be equivalent to a price reduction, making the import substitute cheaper than the import. The desired effect of price reduction would be to drive the imported item off the ghetto market. This procedure would be entirely consistent with a community-owned corporation, since one purpose of the corporation is to add profits as well as wages to the income of ghetto residents. Such profits could be paid in the form of dividends on specific purchases as well as dividends out of general earnings.

The leakage of wages in the ghetto will also be avoided if wage expenditures on ghetto-produced goods and services are sufficient out of total ghetto expenditures to cover the supply price of all stages of production in the ghetto. This means there will be no leakage of wages, if out of aggregate ghetto expenditures a sufficient amount is spent on ghetto-produced goods at the expense of imported goods to equal the aggregate supply price of ghetto-produced goods.

## Market and Product Differentiation

A ghetto income expenditure model based upon a system of black community monopoly is highly compatible with an already established and highly differentiated black consumer market. This market has a unique set of attributes that differentiate the products purchased, the nature of demand conditions, and the prices paid. These distinctive Negro market attributes will combine to impose serious restrictions upon leakage: (1) The nature of black consumer decisions as differentiated by the personal and social value system. (2) Spatial location as delineated by price differences and by a segregated residential-commercial area where almost all purchases are made by Negro customers, and where two-thirds of aggregate Negro spending occurs. (3) Economic location as defined by the black consumers' position on a composite demand curve of all buyers of many specific items of durable and nondurable consumer goods. (4) The shape of black consumers' demand curve for many specific items as differentiated from that of the white consumers' in terms of price elasticity of demand. (5) The pattern of aggregate consumption as defined by differences between black and white consumers in the per dollar allocation of disposable income among the various categories of consumer goods.

This list of Negro market attributes shows that the Negro market is highly differentiated and thus conducive to monopoly control because: (a) black consumers are not indifferent as to whom they buy from; (b) products purchased are differentiated in the mind of black consumers; and (c) black consumers do not have perfect knowledge and are not driven by such knowledge to buy at lower prices outside the black community.

## GHETTO MARKET DEMAND

### Black Consumer Decisions

The black consumer's decisions, as indicated above, are differentiated from those of white consumers by the black's system of personal and social values. Today, a basic element in this system of personal and social values is a need for black awareness and black identity. This is the psychological and cohesive element among individual black consumers and serves as a basic guide as to whom to buy from and how to differentiate the product in terms of the value system. Entwined with the black ghetto consumer's need for black awareness and black identity is his need to compensate for a sense of self-depreciation and powerlessness brought on by an inferior role in the economic life of the community. This explains his demand for black power through a system of black community control. Also, in a system of black power, these fundamental drives for black identity and black power will undoubtedly explain: (1) the individual system of consumer preferences vis-à-vis goods produced in the ghetto community and those produced outside; (2) the price one is willing to pay relative to the price of imported goods; (3) the qualitative aspects of the demand; and (4) the means by which the black consumer can be most effectively sold. That is, a "Buy Black" program would no doubt prove highly effective in the black ghettos of the country today.

### Spatial Attributes of the Market

Spatially, the black ghetto market may be defined as representing roughly the core area of central city. In cities selected for the Model Cities Program, the Model Cities areas represent a good approximation of the spatial limits of the ghetto market area. Analyzing the Model Cities Area (roughly), one census of core area business[4] showed preliminary results that demonstrate: 26.3 percent of the customers of black-owned businesses live mostly in the immediate

[4] *Census of Core Area Businesses,* Eleanor Andreason, Project Director. Preliminary Results, Survey Research Unit (Buffalo, New York, University of Buffalo, 1969).

neighborhood, and 65.3 percent represent a little bit of both; 97.5 percent of the customers of black-owned businesses live in the core area under study. This same study also shows that 50 percent of black-owned businesses report that 90–99 percent of their customers are black.

Assuming that these results are typical of black ghetto markets, we may say that spatially the market of a black-owned economy would be a market area within the core area of the central city, where almost all the buyers are black, a substantial percentage live in the immediate neighborhood, and almost all live in the core area.

*Monopolist Elements.* The localized character of the ghetto market demand lends a monopolistic element to sellers in capturing ghetto purchasing power. The extent of this spatial monopolistic element is evidenced by area price differentials between ghetto area and the more affluent suburban areas. An illustration of the exercise of local area monopoly power is shown in Figure 9-1.

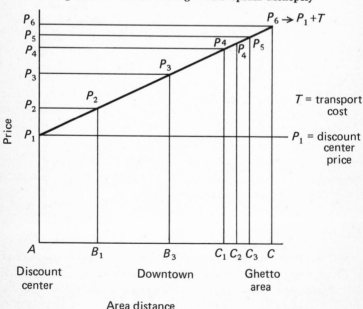

Figure 9-1.  Ghetto Pricing Under Spatial Monopoly

It is assumed that the lowest price is charged in the discount and modern shopping centers located in the suburban areas, designated as $A$. The price prevailing there is indicated by $AP_1$ or the line $P_1P_1$. The ghetto buyer has the option of buying at the lower suburban price, but this involves a transportation cost. For simplicity, transportation cost is assumed to be a linear function of distance. In the graph, it is shown as a 45° line. In reality, however, consumer transportation cost is likely to be a step function. To the ghetto buyer at point $C$, for instance, the real cost of buying from the discount area is $AP_6$, including $AP_1$ (discount center price) plus $P_1P_6$ (transportation cost). In the same way, the real cost of buying from the downtown shopping center, where price is assumed to be somewhat more than the discount center price, is $AP_3$. If, for simplicity, we assumed that buyers are evenly distributed, are indifferent to whom they buy from, and have identical income levels, the seller in the ghetto would charge a price midway between $P_3$ and $P_6$, say $P_4$, rather than the full monopoly price of $AP_6$ or $CP_6$. Otherwise, all buyers living in areas to the left of the point $C$ would shift their purchases downtown where the monopoly price when added to the transport cost would still be less than the monopoly price at $C$.

It may be noted that when the seller charges the price $AP_4$, he again loses all customers to the left of $C_1$.

If he still reduces the price to attract these customers, his marginal revenue will fall because of price reduction to buyers to the right of $C_1$. A more realistic assumption would be that in general white buyers do not come to the ghetto; the potential market area for the ghetto seller would not extend all the way down to $C$ from $C_1$, but would be confined to, say, from $C$ to $C_2$ where the ghetto area ends. In that case, the ghetto seller would be charging a price $C_3P_5$ midway between $CP_6$ and $C_2P'_4$. We thus see that the ghetto seller is in a position to charge a price higher than a pure spatial monopoly model would dictate. He derives this extra monopoly power from the racial factors in the ghetto market.

*Preventing Leakage.* The existence of a local ghetto spatial monopoly price indicates that leakage of ghetto purchasing power is substantially prevented by time and transportation costs involved in seeking lower downtown prices, or lower prices in suburban discount houses. Thus, we may say that the product of black sellers, under a black monopoly system, would be spatially differentiated from that of white sellers in other local markets. This type of product differentiation prevents leakage, even if the ghetto price is higher, or even if the product is an import substitute item.

## The Ghetto Demand Curve

In this section, we will look at black consumer demand entirely from the point of view of the supply side (individual business firms producing and selling a product in the black ghetto market). The concept of the firm here is that of a black community corporation producing an import substitute item. What will be the demand or sales curve of such a corporation?

In the preceding sections, we have already indicated that the product sold in the ghetto market is not homogeneous, but is differentiated by racial and spatial factors. For these reasons, products produced outside the ghetto are not readily substitutable for products produced in the ghetto. To the extent that products produced outside the ghetto are not good substitutes, the ghetto market situation becomes monopolistic vis-à-vis sellers of the product produced outside the ghetto. Thus, the demand curve faced by the individual ghetto producer in a black monopoly system would slope downward. That is, at any given price, black consumers, under conditions of black community differentiation, would be attached to the particular black community product. Under such a demand situation, the ghetto producer through advertising would be able to control black community demand, prices, and output. Such influence would tend to countervail the leakage problem.

## Pattern and Scope of Demand

The pattern of the schedule of black consumer demand for various categories of goods defines the scope of a black power system of ghetto production. This black community demand pattern, which is differentiated from that of white consumers, represents the most urgent set of consumer preferences of a black power economy. An indication of this uniquely black community demand preference is shown by a comparison of the way the black community allocates its disposable income with the way white consumers do.

It is observable from Table 9-1 that, relative to white consumers, the black community places a very high premium upon (for example) the consumer category of personal care. Clothing, among nondurables, and house furnishings, equipment, and housing, among durables, are especially valued. An example of black community expenditures in the personal care category is shown by Negro expenditures on cosmetics in Table 9-2.

Personal care items, as well as many of the items falling in the first ten consumer categories, offer the ghetto producer a ready-made market situation for black community product differentiation. In such a demand situation, a downward sloping demand curve facing the ghetto producer may readily be shifted to the right (increase in sales) by ghetto producer advertising. In this case, the problem of leakage would become minimal.

There is other empirical evidence of the possibility of the ghetto producer facing an upward shifting demand curve for items

Table 9-1. Market Demand Differentials Between Black and White Urban Families According to the Allocation of Disposable Income

|  | Negro families spend: |
| --- | --- |
| 1. All food | 4% more |
| 2. Food at home | 7.3% more |
| 3. Tobacco | 29.4% more |
| 4. Alcoholic beverages | 25.0% more |
| 5. Housing | 7.1% more |
| 6. Household operations | 3.4% more |
| 7. House furnishing and equipment | 8.0% more |
| 8. Clothing | 22.5% more |
| 9. Personal care | 36.0% more |
| 10. Travel, other than auto | 29.4% more |
| 11. Food away from home | 9.9% less |
| 12. Medical care | 28.4% less |
| 13. Recreation | 14.6% less |
| 14. Reading | 11.0% less |
| 15. Education | 50.0% less |
| 16. Transportation | 22.0% less |

Source: Based on U.S. Dept. of Labor, Bureau of Labor Statistics, BLS Report No. 237, No. 238 (July 1964).

Table 9-2.    Cosmetics Expenditures in the United States

|  | Total U.S. | Total Negro |
|---|---|---|
| Stick and roll-on deodorant | $ 50,090,000 | $ 4,257,650 |
| Spray deodorant | 149,310,000 | 13,437,900 |
| Cream deodorant | 32,800,000 | 5,313,600 |
| Eye makeup | 88,500,000 | 4,956,000 |
| Cleansing cream and lotions | 242,820,000 | 21,368,160 |
| Face makeup base, liquid | 59,340,000 | 2,848,320 |
| Face powder, loose | 26,380,000 | 2,743,520 |
| Face powder, pressed | 61,680,000 | 3,885,840 |
| Hair coloring products | 205,520,000 | 12,331,200 |
| Hair shampoo | 247,000,000 | 20,055,600 |
| Creme rinse | 22,770,000 | 1,115,730 |
| Hair spray | 265,000,000 | 9,275,000 |
| Hand cream | 16,950,000 | 1,440,750 |
| Hand lotion | 49,640,000 | 4,815,080 |
| Nail polish | 62,200,000 | 4,976,000 |
| Perfume, cologne, and toilet water | 241,990,000 | 20,811,140 |
| Lipstick | 217,560,000 | 16,099,440 |
| Bath powder (talcum) | 46,630,000 | 3,870,290 |
| Bath oil | 40,730,000 | 3,543,510 |

Source: Total spending in all outlets: "Brand Rating Index, 1968," Drug Trade News (August 5, 1968).

especially demanded by the black community. In cities of over 500,000 where the black population represents 25 percent of the population, black consumer consumption of certain food items over the period of a year exceeds 40 percent of total consumption.[5] This evidence suggests that in large cities at any given time, a substantial space on a composite demand schedule of all buyers of a given item may represent black consumers. A process of breaking down such a composite demand curve by black community product differentiation by advertising would make it possible for the ghetto producer of the item to face an upward shifting demand curve. In the case of food items and many personal care items that are

[5] See Market Research Corporation of America, data covering period from January through December, 1964. The data show that Negroes consumed 41.5 percent of the total pounds of all-purpose flour, 43.0 percent of the total cases of syrup and 34 percent of the total pounds of frozen vegetables.

almost always purchased in the local ghetto neighborhood, such a possibility seems imminent.

We may conclude this analysis of the problem of leakage of wage receipts from ghetto production by saying that limits to leakage are set by six factors: (1) the nature of and motivations behind individual black consumer decisions; (2) the racial and spatial factors that differentiate both the market and products sold therein; (3) the nature of the demand curve facing the ghetto producer; (4) the special pattern of black community consumer demand that is highly compatible with a locally-owned market supply system; (5) evidence of the possibility of upward shifting ghetto consumer demand schedules faced by ghetto producers for the pattern of consumer preferences most desired by black consumers; and (6) the possibility of purchase dividends for ghetto buying of selected items that may be purchased outside the ghetto.

It is assumed, of course, that the efficiency of the black monopoly will be at least equal to that of white enterprises and that, other things being equal, black consumers will purchase goods from the ghetto economy rather than from outside. Also, profits will go to ghetto residents in the form of dividends. The greater the profitable sales, the greater the dividends.

## INDUSTRY MIX IN THE GHETTO

Within the limits of ghetto consumer demand, the community-owned monopolist should be able to set the pattern of ghetto market production in terms of: (a) the economics of various forms of production operations in the ghetto; (b) the economic feasibility of various types of enterprises within each productive form; and (c) the most economical (in terms of comparative advantage considerations) combination of various types of enterprises.

### Production Operations

In terms of the actual business institutions in which people are associated in their production operations, there are six basic forms of production: (1) manufacturing and mechanical industries, including factory work, construction, and hand trades other than construction (tailoring, millinery and dressmaking, dyeing and cleaning, laundering, shoe repairing, watch repairing, and so forth); (2) transportation and communication; (3) storage; (4) merchandizing and trade; (5) household production, including direct personal services; and (6) other personal service including barber shops, beauty shops, custodial services, food service hotels, and the like.

The forms of production operations in the ghetto extend from a limited amount of construction work to beauty and barber shops, and include very little factory work. We may hypothesize that the level of aggregate gross sales in the ghetto is influenced by (1) the form of ghetto production operations and (2) the actual distribution of the population of business units by form of production operations.

Incomes vary in these forms of production operations because of differences in the aggregate value of output. The average value of output of a factory would be greater than in a barber shop. Barber shop investment yields less in aggregate value of output than the same amount of aggregate investment in a factory. This difference will be due to limitations in output imposed by the size of each individual barber shop compared with the size of a factory. Thus, we may say that the output per unit of capital in a factory is greater than the output per unit of capital in a barber shop. Also, the aggregate gross sales from a given amount of capital invested in barber shops will be less than the aggregate gross sales from the same amount of capital investment in factories.

When we observe the black ghetto community, however, we observe that the actual distribution of the population of black-owned business units is concentrated in those forms of production operations that (a) permit the entry of small business units and (b) set limitations upon the aggregate volume of gross sales in relation to the aggregate volume of capital investment. That is, the same amount of aggregate capital investment with a different distribution of business units by form of production operation would raise the aggregate level of gross sales in the ghetto.

Some evidence for this is shown in Table 9-3, which shows the percentage distribution of black-owned and white-owned business units in the core area of Buffalo, classified according to form of production. Using the percentage distribution of black-owned as a

Table 9-3.  Percentage Distribution of Black-Owned and White-Owned
Business Units in the Core Area of Buffalo, N.Y.,
According to Form of Production

| Form of production | Distribution of business units | | Index of white relative to black (Black = 100) |
|---|---|---|---|
| | Black-owned 100 | White-owned 100 | |
| Factory | 1.5 | 11.0 | 733 |
| Construction | 0.8 | 3.1 | 362 |
| Hand trade | | | |
| Drycleaners | 3.5 | 2.7 | 77 |
| Auto and other repairs | 6.7 | 7.0 | 104 |
| Merchandising | | | |
| Wholesale | 1.5 | 8.4 | 560 |
| Retail | 46.8 | 54.0 | 113 |
| Transportation | 1.0 | 2.7 | 270 |
| Services | | | |
| Beauty and barber shops | 26.3 | 2.2 | 8 |
| Other services | 11.7 | 8.4 | 72 |
| Unclassified | .2 | .5 | |

Source: Census of Core Area Businesses, Eleanor Andreason, Project Director
(Buffalo, N.Y.: State University of New York, 1969).

base (black-owned = 100), the table shows an index of difference in
the form of the two distributions.

We observe that in factory work the white-owned business units
are more than seven times that of black-owned; in construction,
white-owned is almost four times black-owned; and in wholesale,
there are almost six times more white-owned than black-owned
operations. For barber and beauty shops, however, the index of
white-owned relative to black-owned business is only 8 percent.

With respect to the distribution of gross sales among the black-
owned and white-owned business units, we observe from this data
that 52.5 percent of white-owned businesses had gross sales in excess
of $50,000; and only 14 percent of black-owned businesses exceeded
$50,000 in gross sales.

The difference in the distribution of gross sales between the
black-owned and white-owned population of business units in the
Buffalo ghetto results in a big difference in average gross receipts,
which is $47,000 for white-owned and only $8,000 for black-owned
businesses. This difference is undoubtedly due partly to differences

in the predominant form of business institutions among the two groups and partly to differences in the patterns of the two distributions. For example, although 46.8 percent of black-owned business units in the Buffalo ghetto are in retail merchandising, only 1.5 percent of black-owned businesses are engaged in wholesale merchandising. This case is typical of the black ghettos throughout the country.

A community-owned monopolist, faced with a downward sloping demand curve, may set the level of aggregate gross sales in the ghetto by determining the level of output of the various forms of business operations and by rationalizing the population of business units by form of business. The rationalization of business units is not merely a matter of dealing with the quantitative distribution of the population of business units but involves the problem of the most economical combination of ghetto enterprises, which will be discussed later in this chapter.

## Feasibility of Ghetto Manufacturing: A Case Study

The range of economic feasibility of ghetto labor-using enterprises could be expanded by developing a manufacturing sector within the ghetto community. The range of economic feasibility would widen to include the prospects for vertical integration of the various stages of production for manufacturing to wholesaling and to retailing. Each stage of production would have its relative impact on employment and wages within the ghetto. The economic effects of vertical integration of the various stages of production within the ghetto would be the equivalent of generating, in addition to the labor export sector, two additional sectors: a capital goods sector consisting of manufacturing operations and a consumer goods sector consisting of wholesale and retail operations all functioning within a circuit flow of money and goods within the ghetto.

## Ghetto Supply Costs

Our concept of the economic feasibility of ghetto manufacturing enterprises is a consumer demand concept rather than cost concept. Output determines per unit costs, but consumer demand determines output, and price determines consumer demand. Thus, *price* times the *quantity* black consumers are willing to take is the factor that sets the limits of economic feasibility and determines the relevant supply costs of ghetto producers. The capital supply cost and the value added at all stages may be derived by working backward from retail sales (*P* times *Q*) in the black consumer market.

Those commodities for which the retail sales potential is greatest among black consumers represent the greatest potential for manufacturing enterprises. Illustrative of the retail sales potential for ghetto manufacturing, shown in Table 9-4, are the average annual expenditures of urban families and single consumers for certain selected items. Comparison of average annual expenditures among black and white families will show not only the absolute amount spent by black families, but also the ratios of purchase rates of black and white families.

The index of Negro expenditures to white in the last column of Table 9-4 are ratios of purchase rates of Negro versus white relative to the ratio of their average annual expenditures as equal to 100. It should be noted that furniture, clothing, and personal care supplies are the greatest prospect for a ghetto manufacturing monopolist. These indexes may form the basis for determining the best pattern

Table 9-4. Average Annual Negro and White Expenditures of Negro Versus White, with Indexes of Negro to White Expenditures, 1960–65

| Items of average annual expenditures | Family annual expenditures white | Family annual expenditures Negro | Index of Negro to white expenditures |
|---|---|---|---|
| Average annual expenditure for current consumption | $5,333.00 | $3,685.00 | 100.0 |
| Appliances | 78.00 | 58.00 | 107.0 |
| Furniture | 80.00 | 65.00 | 117.0 |
| Clothing and accessories | 534.00 | 446.00 | 119.0 |
| Men's and boys' clothing | 194.00 | 159.00 | 117.0 |
| Women's, girls' and infants' clothing | 271.00 | 227.00 | 119.0 |
| Materials and services | 69.00 | 61.00 | 126.00 |
| Personal care | 150.00 | 141.00 | 126.00 |
| Supplies | 82.00 | 69.00 | 119.00 |
| Food | 1,296.00 | 960.00 | 106.00 |

*Source:* National Industrial Conference Board, *Expenditure Patterns of the American Family, 1960–65* (based on U.S. Dept. of Labor data).

of ghetto manufacturing enterprises. By working backward from the retail stage through the wholesale stage to the manufacturing stage, one may determine the following:

1. Current differences in size (value of assets) of establishments with respect to minimum capital requirements in terms of profitability.

2. The capital supply cost at the manufacturing stage (that part of value added by manufacturers representing return to capital) per dollar of retail sales in the ghetto.

3. The total capital requirements at the munfacturing stage for the given amount of retail sales in the ghetto.

4. The amount of employment at the manufacturing stage (employment rate per dollar of capital investment) for the given amount of retail sales in the ghetto.

5. The amount of wage income (wage portion of value added by manufacturers) per dollar of capital requirement at the manufacturing stage for a given dollar of retail sales in the ghetto.

6. Differentials at the manufacturing level for a given dollar of retail sales in the ghetto among the various types of enterprises facing the most favorable demand conditions.

7. Value productivity of capital investment, that is, rate of return on capital.

8. Labor capital ratio, that is, a given amount of capital required to sustain a given amount of employment.

On the basis of the above criteria, the industry mix of the ghetto could be determined with respect to the most promising types of enterprises for vertical integration in the ghetto and the amount of capital requirements and labor force consistent with sales in the ghetto.

## Vertical Integration

We shall consider the possibility of vertical integration of all stages of production by a ghetto monopoly corporation. The ghetto monopolist confronts a substantial consumer demand that is (1) influenced by racial and cultural factors and (2) spatially delineated by a traditional social system of racial segregation.

Within the spatial confines of the ghetto areas of the United States, we have estimated that the aggregate income is $12 billion. Credit purchases and purchases from welfare receipts are estimated to add about 70 percent to ghetto purchasing power. How far can a ghetto monopolist go in capturing this purchasing power by integrating the manufacturing stages with subsequent wholesale-retail distribution?

If all ghetto consumer income is spent in the ghetto, a community monopolist could avoid leakage by supplying only ghetto-produced commodities. Likewise, if any given category of consumer goods is purchased only in the ghetto or, if the average amount budgeted for these goods out of ghetto income is spent only in the ghetto, leakage could be avoided by supplying only ghetto-produced goods. Thus a basic yardstick for setting limits on leakage is the extent to which the item is purchased in the ghetto area. A clear-cut example of this would be housing. Housing services produced in the ghetto would, of course, be purchased in the ghetto up to the amount budgeted for housing. Clothing is another example. We are selecting clothing because the black urban family spends 22.5 percent more of its dollar for clothing than white urban families (see Table 9-1); and also that the index of purchase rates (Table 9-4) for clothing and accessories is 19 percent higher for black families compared with white families.

Therefore, taking clothing as our prime example, we shall consider: (a) the aggregate amount budgeted by ghetto residents; (b) whether the budgeted amount is spent in the ghetto; and (c) the economic feasibility (in terms of the volume of capital required, return to labor, capital/output ratio and so forth) of vertically integrating all stages of production, based upon the Newark data.

First, we observe from data already shown in Chapter 3, that $12 billion is expended. This is shown in the Figure 9-2 chart below, which represents the minimum market potential for ghetto monopoly enterprises.

The arrows show an estimate of aggregate ghetto consumer expenditures out of existing aggregate ghetto incomes without reference as to whether these expenditures occurred within or outside the ghetto area. Since it is the objective, however, of a ghetto monopoly to capture this aggregate sales potential the question is:

Figure 9-2. Aggregate Initial Sales Potential of a Black Ghetto Monopoly

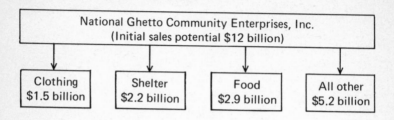

Can this sales potential be captured through vertical integration of all stages of production (retail, wholesale, and manufacturing) for all categories of consumer expenditures? Or, can all stages be captured for some consumer categories and some stages for other categories of consumer expenditures?

## Clothing Budgets in the Ghetto

Figure 9-2 shows that ghetto residents spend $1.5 billion, or 13 percent of income on clothing. We have estimates from the data in our Newark study that a three-year average (1965–67) of total gross sales of clothing in unincorporated [6] Newark ghetto stores was $14,139,340. This amounts to 11.1 percent of total Newark ghetto income of $127 million.

The Newark data indicate that clothing purchases in Newark ghetto stores, amounting to 11 percent of income, comprise almost the entire clothing budget. Or that of the total clothing budget, the amount spent for clothing inside the Newark ghetto approximates the national ghetto average of 13 percent of income budgeted for clothing. If this is the general case, it is feasible for the ghetto monopolists to capture the entire $1.5 billion of aggregate ghetto expenditures at the retail stage. This would provide a good possibility of avoiding leakage, assuming there is vertical integration with the manufacturing stage. The economic feasibility of vertical integration of the retail stage with earlier stages in clothing production is our next consideration.

[6] Data not available for sales in incorporated stores. However, in Table 9-5, we have estimated total clothing sales as $21.5 million.

## From Retailing to Manufacturing

Recall that in our input-output model discussed in Chapter 7 (see Table 7-1) we demonstrated the intersectoral flow of resources in a three-sector labor-intensive ghetto economy, using hypothetical data. In the same model we shall now use actual data in representing clothing purchases in the Newark ghetto for the year 1967. Working backward from known ghetto sales, we will attempt to determine the overall capital/output ratio resulting from vertical integration of all stages of clothing production. We can also find values, at the manufacturing stage, of: (a) capital requirements for the given level of ghetto sales; (b) capital/wage ratio; (c) capital/income ratio; (d) rate of return on capital; and (e) capital supply cost per dollar of retail sales. To arrive at these values we have extrapolated to ghetto figures from national manufacturing and retail data on the apparel industry as contained in the *Economic Almanac, 1967–68.*[7] We followed certain procedures and made certain assumptions:

1. All figures from which ratios are computed relate to the year 1963, except where specified.

2. The wholesale stage has been skipped as a distinct stage because it is assumed that both manufacturing and retailing will take place within the confines of the ghetto. In this case wholesaling and retailing would represent a single operation in ghetto distribution.

3. Operating expenses are derived from comparative figures for the wholesale business; that is, ratios of wholesale operating expenses to wholesale sales are used.

4. The capital stock for retailing is derived from the national sales/assets ratio (2.06).

5. Profits are gross (of tax).

6. Value added by manufacturing = wages + profits + operating expenses; retail sales = cost of goods sold + value added. This equation presumes that all operating expenses are received by ghetto dwellers. This procedure does not take into account the multiplier effect of these expenditures, which presumably is very great where savings are small, as in the ghetto.

[7] National Industrial Conference Board, *Economic Almanac, 1967–1968.*

Table 9-5.  A Model of Manufacturing Feasibility Based upon Known
Sales, Newark, New Jersey, 1967, Showing the Intersectoral Flow
of Resources Generated by Manufacturing in Three-Sector
Labor-Intensive Ghetto Economy Such as Newark

| | Capital goods sector; manu-facturing (wearing apparel) | Consumer goods sector; wholesale-retail (wearing apparel) | Labor export sector; labor employ-ment outside the black community | Value of output |
|---|---|---|---|---|
| Capital imports | | | | |
| Borrowed capital | ($3,700,000) | | | |
|  a) Machines (Annual cap-ital costs) | 221,000 | | | $    221,000 |
|  b) Raw material | 4,700,000 | | | 4,700,000 |
|  c) Stock, merchandise | | ($9,600,000)* | | |
| Wages | 2,616,000 | 2,300,000 | $4,921,000 | 9,837,000 |
| Profits | 418,000 | 217,137 | | 635,137 |
| Operating expenses | 1,645,000 | 4,500,000 | | 6,145,000 |
| Value of output (Sales) | $9,600,000 | $7,017,137 | $4,921,000 | 21,538,137 |
| Payments for imports | | | $4,921,000 | −4,921,000 |
| Net value of output in Newark ghetto | | | | $16,617,137 |

* Excluded to avoid double counting.

7. Extrapolation to ghetto figures from national data is performed by using the latest ghetto figure of retail sales of apparel
in the Newark ghetto, which was for the year 1967, as reported by
the Internal Revenue Service on the basis of a probability sample
of stores submitted for data. National data are all computed from
the *Economic Almanac*.[8]

On the basis of the above procedures and assumptions, and
working backward from a known estimate of $16,708,502 as repre-
senting apparel expenditures in the Newark ghetto during 1967, we
have constructed Table 9-5. The table shows what would have been
the intersectoral flow of Newark ghetto resources in meeting its own

[8] *Economic Almanac*, 1967–1968.

demand for clothing by engaging in clothing manufacturing. Several observations can be made from the data in Table 9-5:

1. The total output of clothing was $21,538,000.
2. The net value of output of clothing was $16,617,000.
3. The capital goods sector (manufacturing operations) would have bought its machines and raw materials from outside the Newark ghetto.
4. The value of imports of machines and raw materials ($4,921,-000) would have been paid for by the export of $4,921,000 worth of labor. This would have involved the export of 1,537 unemployed Newark ghetto workers at a minimum wage of $1.60 per hour for 50 weeks. Out of a Newark ghetto (core area) labor force of 26,987 during 1967,[9] new jobs would have been required for 5.6 percent of the labor force, or roughly one-half of the unemployed in 1967. Alternatively, the 23,614 people already fully employed during 1967 would have needed an average raise in pay of only $2.08 per worker. Of course, any combination of new jobs for the unemployed and pay raises for the employed that would yield $4,921,000 would complete the swap of black labor for white capital.
5. The capital goods sector is vertically integrated with the consumer goods sector (distribution operations).
6. The money value of the purchases for the distribution operations in the consumer goods sector must, of course, equal the output of the manufacturing operations in the capital goods sector.
7. There is no producer goods sector. All producer goods are imported and paid for out of earnings from otherwise unemployed labor exported to the white community.
8. The export sector is the balancing factor for general equilibrium. Since this Newark ghetto economy does not produce its own machines and raw materials for manufacturing, it would run a deficit in its trade balance and would have to cut back $4,921,000 on capital purchases or make up the deficit by exports that do not require machines for its production. Export of labor (1,537 unemployed workers at a minimum wage of $1.60) bringing in wages

[9] Research Section, Rutgers University, Population and Labor Force, Newark, N.J., Spring, 1966, p. 10.

of $4,921,000 would wipe out the import deficit, and the economy would be in equilibrium.

9. In terms of our earlier ghetto production function, observe that $Y = L_E$ ($4,921,000) $+ L_K$ ($5,556,137) $+ L_D$ ($4,916,000) $=$ $15,393,137 +$ (operating expenses ($6,145,000) $=$ $21,538,137).

10. The total value added in the ghetto community (wages $+$ profits) at all stages was $5,551,137.

11. $4,921,000 earned outside the ghetto and converted to capital within the ghetto generated a net value of output of $16,617,000. Thus, the output/capital ratio, $\dfrac{\$16,617,000}{\$\,4,921,000} = 3.4$. That is, $1.00 of borrowed capital would yield $3.40 in net value output.

12. The rate of return on borrowed capital at the manufacturing stage is computed as follows: profits ($418,000) $\div$ borrowed capital ($3,700,000) $=$ 11.3 percent.

13. The capital/wage ratio was 1.0004 compared with an overall national capital/wage ratio of 1.40789.

14. The capital/income ratio was 1.21 compared with an overall national capital/income ratio of 1.006.

15. The capital supply cost at the manufacturing stage (that part of value added by manufacturing representing return to capital per dollar of retail clothing sales) in the Newark ghetto, $418,000 (profits) $\div$ $16,617,000 (retail sales) $=$ 0.025. That is, for every dollar of retail sales of clothing, 2.5 cents in profits would be created at the manufacturing stage. If we apply this ratio, (0.025) to the percent aggregate ghetto purchases of clothing throughout the country, which we estimate to be $1.8 billion, aggregate ghetto profits at the manufacturing stage for clothing would amount to $27 million annually.

16. We note from Table 9-5 that wages of $2,616,000 would be generated at the manufacturing stage in the Newark ghetto, representing 15.7 percent of sales (the net value of output from all stages $=$ $16,617,000). If we apply this percentage (15.7) to aggregate U.S. clothing purchases of ghetto residents ($1.5 billion) the amount that would go to wages at the manufacturing stage would be $235.5 million, and if we assume a minimum annual wage of $3,200 per worker, this would permit the employment of 73,593 workers in clothing manufacturing alone. This amount of employment in clothing manufacturing would use up 12.3 percent of the 600,000 (Negro

and other nonwhite races) unemployed in 1969.[10] In terms of total wages at all stages, the percentage of total wages (all stages) of total net value (sales) was 29.76 percent; and, if we apply this percentage to aggregate ghetto clothing purchases, the amount that would go to ghetto wages as a result of vertical integration of clothing production in the ghetto would be ($1.5 billion $\times$ 0.2976), which equals $446,400,000. This amount would permit the annual employment of 139,500 unemployed workers at $3,200,[11] representing 23.2 percent of the total unemployed black workers in 1969.

17. If we assume that these wage receipts ($446,400,000) from vertical integration of ghetto clothing production had a multiplier of 1 (no saving), this amount after initially adding to aggregate ghetto income for the given year would be continuously respent. Therefore, in each subsequent year, ghetto aggregate income would rise by $446.4 million assuming no change in the current aggregate ghetto clothing purchases of $1.5 billion. But current aggregate ghetto purchases of clothing will rise as the ghetto population and income grow. If we assume that the current Negro population of 22.3 million will grow by 2 percent, the Negro population in ten years (1980) will be 27.2 million;[12] or 5.2 million more than 1969. And if 55 percent of this additional population live in central cities, there will be 2.75 million more Negroes in central cities by 1980. If, as at present, $1,450 is the future per capita income of Negroes in central city ghettos, and, as at present, 13 percent of ghetto income is spent for clothing, per capita clothing expenditure will be $188.50. This amount, when multiplied by 2.75 million additional Negroes in central cities, gives a total additional $518,375,000 to be spent for clothing by central cities (ghetto) residents by 1980. If we divide this $518,375,000 by ten, we get an annual aggregate increment to clothing purchases by ghetto residents of $51.8 million. Over the ten years, this gives a growth rate of 2.9 percent in ghetto clothing purchases.

Since wages would represent 29.76 percent of the additional $518,375,000 in total ghetto purchases, the annual wage increment

[10] U.S. Department of Commerce, *Current Population Reports,* Series P-23, No. 29, *Bureau of Labor Statistics Report* No. 375; 1969.

[11] Figure $3,200 used for estimating purposes.

[12] 1.218 $\times$ 22.3 million.

from vertical integration of clothing production in ghetto economies would be $15.4 million over the ten-year period, representing a growth rate in wages of roughly 3 percent.

*Expenditures on Shelter.* In an earlier chart, it was shown that of the $12 billion spent in the ghetto, $2.2 billion goes for shelter. Obviously, housing services produced in the ghetto are directly consumed in the ghetto. In this case, the entire amount of $2.2 billion annually would go to the black community corporation, the sole owner of all rental dwellings. All construction work, repairs, and so forth would also be performed by the black community monopoly.

*When Vertical Integration Is Not Feasible.* If we use the Newark ghetto as an example, establishment of a black community corporate monopoly in wholesaling and retailing of the existing volume of ghetto business would yield to ghetto households (in the form of factor payments), an increase of $5.4 billion, 44.9 percent of their present income of $12 billion. This would represent an increase of 1,343 percent in factor returns to ghetto households. The figure is derived from Table 3-16, which shows that factor payments (wages, profits, rents, and dividends) going to the white enclave sector of the Newark ghetto amount to $55,828,000; or 44.9 percent of Newark ghetto income, flowing to white owners of wholesale and retail establishments. The table shows that the present black-owned business sector receives from the factor payments only 1.8 percent of gross sales while the white-owned sector receives 25.6 percent. Black monopoly of the existing volume of business in the Newark ghetto would raise the factor payments of the black sector from $3,867,500 to $55,828,000, an increase of 1,343 percent.

It is clear that the mere transfer of ownership of the wholesale and retail stages of ghetto enterprises to a community-owned black monopoly corporation would be highly significant purely on the basis of the existing volume of ghetto business. In the Newark case, the factor payments now going to the white community would provide each Newark ghetto family with an income of $2,195.

By taking the existing volume of sales as a target, it is feasible to expand the income of the black community by including the manufacturing stage for many items, as shown by clothing—undoubtedly for personal care items—furniture, and perhaps dairy products, bakeries, paints, and many items of household operation. All of this would, of course, become more feasible within the financial structure of a community-owned ghetto monopoly corporation.

*Ghetto Retail Sales Potential.* The concept of the volume of ghetto retail sales to be met by feasible ghetto manufacturing enterprises under community monopoly is, of course, not limited to the existing level of sales under the present size of ghetto business units. In the analysis of the feasibility of clothing manufacturers in the Newark ghetto we used the existing level of retail sales in order to demonstrate feasibility based upon a known demand. This procedure is useful for production planning, but the demand and sales potential of the ghetto undoubtedly exceed the present actual volume. This is the case because the fixed and working capital of many of the firms are inadequate even for the present size of the ghetto market.

The economics of the size of ghetto establishments must be based upon a projection of gross profits with respect to population data, buying habits, and purchase rates of ghetto consumers compared with the performance of other markets of the same products. Utilization of such marketing information in ghetto capital planning would fall within the capacity of a community-owned monopolist because of its greater borrowing capacity. In estimating manufacturing feasibility by working backwards as we have shown from sales at the retail stage to determine capital costs at the manufacturing stage, the community-owned monopolist could start from a maximum condition of retail sales potential.

An indication of gross sales potential that would accrue to a black-owned corporate monopoly in a ghetto market is shown by a comparison between the black-owned sole proprietorship sector and the white-owned corporate wholesale and retail sector in the ghetto.

Table 3-6 indicates that on the basis of the existing corporate gross sales in the Newark ghetto, a black community-owned corporate monopoly could raise the investment and sales level of the existing black-owned sector by more than 600 percent, and the wage bill per establishment could be raised by almost 1,200 percent. Also, the investment/wage ratio would fall from $4.80 of capital to $1.00 of wages, to $2.50 of capital per $1.00 of wages, a 48 percent reduction.

The foregoing illustration indicates that the approach to economic feasibility at the manufacturing stage in terms of maximum sales per business unit at the retail stage may require relatively large capital expenditures. It is unlikely that loans of the required magnitude will be available to individual black business men. Such large capital expenditures, however, are necessary for the maximization of ghetto employment and income per dollar of capital expenditure at all stages of production. What is needed is a broader economic base for borrowing large sums. A community-owned monopolist implies the pooling of all capital assets of the black community as a broad economic base for required capital expansion.

# GHETTO PRODUCTION ORGANIZATION

## The Theory

Our underlying theory of ghetto production is an input-output theory where productivity is defined in terms of labor input capacity. Thus, the productivity of the ghetto is defined as the amount of labor it will absorb, just as the productivity of an acre of land may be defined as the amount of fertilizer it will absorb. Two one-acre pieces of land may have identical net products, but one may require a great deal of fertilizer, and the other utilize a smaller amount of fertilizer more effectively. Now if the price of fertilizer is very cheap relative to land, the output per unit of fertilizer (efficiency) on the acre of land using the smaller amount of fertilizer may not matter much. One may as well use a lower-grade land requiring a great deal of fertilizer.

In the ghetto, labor is cheap relative to capital. So, following the above line of reasoning, it is possible to increase the productivity of the ghetto by maximizing the input of labor with lower-grade labor-using capital. Increasing the output per unit of labor may yield the same net product with less labor, but cause unemployment.

## Production Under Community Monopoly

Theoretically, a private monopolist interested in maximizing profits in the short run will set output at the point where marginal revenue equals short-run marginal costs. This will be some point to the left of the minimum point of the average cost curve. A community-owned monopolist, interested in maximizing employment, will seek to expand the average product of labor by using more and more labor up to the point where the marginal value product of labor is equal to its wage. This is a crucial implication of a black monopoly system because the economics of ghetto production is to maximize the input of labor by economizing on capital and making labor go as far as possible. The underlying supporting principle of production is that whenever any resource is used so heavily that its marginal physical product is near zero or negative, some other resource (or resources) is being used so sparingly that an increase in its quantity relative to other resources will increase the total product. This is shown in Figure 9-3.

Figure 9-3. Stages of Production of Ghetto Labor and Capital

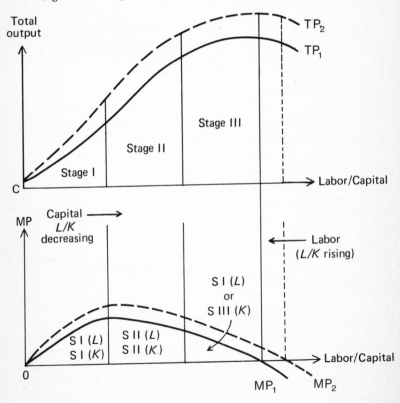

Notice that, with respect to the combination of labor and capital, the ghetto economy is in the third stage in the employment of capital and in the first stage with respect to the employment of labor. That is, under present conditions of ghetto production organization, its labor resources are used so sparingly that the marginal product of labor would rise if more labor is used relative to capital in stage III. The present mercantile (trade) service type of capital in the ghetto is used so heavily that its marginal physical productivity is near zero or probably negative (measured in terms of the high rate of failure and the marginal nature of the all too numerous miniscule enterprises). Noted also that a rise in the marginal physical product in stage I (labor) or stage III (capital) would shift the total product curve of the ghetto upward (as shown by the dotted total product curve) and would be equivalent to technological change.

## The Best Combination of Ghetto Enterprises

*The Problem of Capital Replacement.* Our concept of a single monopoly seller in the ghetto embraces all ghetto enterprises as part of a conglomerate of enterprises. The term enterprises, as used here, does not refer to types of products, but to types of productive activity, such as factory work, construction, hand trades other than construction, merchandising, transportation, and services (including rental of dwelling units). All of these types of productive activity in the ghetto involve in the aggregate a total amount of fixed capital in various stages of economic decline. That is, gross investment minus depreciation in the black ghetto is either zero or less than zero. This problem of capital replacement is usually the kind of problem an industry faces at the end of a long-run period, when the fixed capital cost of the firm becomes variable. It is during the end of such a long-run period that existing capital facilities may be expanded, contracted, or abandoned.

Assuming that this analogy of fixed costs becoming variable is relevant to the present capital structure of the black ghetto, the problem is to determine what new combination of enterprises will replace the existing capital stock. In terms of the large supply of underutilized labor in the ghetto what new combination of ghetto enterprises will: (a) maximize employment; (b) increase the productivity of ghetto labor; and (c) maximize the real income of the ghetto community as a whole?

*Complementary Enterprises.* The applicable principle of ghetto enterprise combination is the principle involved in the complementary relationship between enterprises. This relationship occurs when one enterprise contributes some element of production to another. For example, the community monopolist could produce its own paper, provide laundry service for local barber and beauty shops, do local construction and building maintenance, or produce its own building material.

The more complementary the ghetto enterprises are, the more the ghetto economy approaches some limit of self-sufficiency. Under conditions of perfect competition and full employment, however, self-sufficiency is limited by comparative costs. But since there is an absence of perfect competition and there is unemployment it may pay the community monopolist to produce its own supplies insofar as it can feasibly do so. The limiting factor would not in all cases be the cheaper price of supplies outside the ghetto, but the economic feasibility of production and maximum employment within the ghetto as long as there is unemployed labor. In this respect, it may pay the ghetto monopolist to use its otherwise unemployed labor to produce its own supplies where feasible, rather than buy these supplies at a lower price outside. Since unemployed labor has no opportunity cost, such labor is free to the black community as a whole; to buy supplies outside at a cheaper price is to save socially free labor that would not be utilized at all.

The community-owned monopolist can produce all of its supplies and services for which it has the know-how. It will have a market very close at hand—right in its own establishment.

*Proportions Between Enterprises.* Since capital is the scarce factor, there is the possibility of conflict between enterprises in the use of capital. This raises the question of proportionality in the relative size of various enterprises since it is the combined effect with all of the elements of production that must serve as the criterion of how much capital the monopolist is to allocate to complementary enterprises.

The underlying theory of adjusting the combination of the various enterprises in terms of their relative size is the theory of comparative advantage. Complementary enterprises must be proportioned with the main enterprises on the basis of equalized advantage. That is, the proportion between them and their relative prices must be adjusted to keep them all at equal advantage. A fairly small laundry operation that services the community monopolist may enjoy equal advantage with a paper factory within the monopoly establishment. If the laundry operation becomes too large, however, it will be at a comparative disadvantage with the paper factory. Therefore, the relative size of the laundry and paper factory should be such as to place them at equal advantage.

## PRICING, OUTPUT, AND PRODUCT DISTRIBUTION

### Pricing and Output

Since the objective of the ghetto monopolist is to maximize the input of labor, the level of labor inputs will depend upon the cost-rates of labor and the selling prices of the products. Specifically, the problem is to minimize the level of unemployment subject to constraints such as the production function, the growth of stocks of capital and labor, and competitive returns to factors. The ghetto monopolist will not attempt to set the level of output and price so as to maximize profits. Market prices and wage rates of labor will be taken as given, and the level of output will be arrived at by balancing additional expenses of labor against additional receipts. It will pay to use additional labor as long as the additional product of labor pays for the additional cost of labor.

That is, if we take successive inputs of labor with their respective outputs, we may compute additional labor inputs per unit of additional output; by applying the cost-rates of labor to these additional inputs, we can get the additional labor cost resulting from using another unit of labor per business unit. For example, if one more unit of labor adds four units of output, the additional inputs of labor per unit of additional output is one-fourth or .250. If the cost rate per unit of labor is $16.00, the additional labor costs of using an additional unit of labor is $4.00 per unit of additional output ($16.00 × .250). If another unit of labor adds six units of output, the additional labor costs per unit of additional output is $2.656 per unit of additional output ($16.00 × .166). In carrying this out for various inputs of labor, we will observe a reduction in labor costs per unit of additional output, after which there will be a rising labor cost.

As long as the rising labor costs are covered by the selling price, and no other costs are increased, it will pay the ghetto monopolist to add more labor. Labor will be added up to the point where the curve representing the costs of additional inputs of labor intersects the selling price. This is the *marginal cost approach* of a community-owned monopolist seeking to fully utilize its input capacity for labor. The curve of costs of additional inputs of labor will cut the average cost curve of capital and labor at the point of least cost, but the level of output will be some point to the right of the least cost point on the average cost curve.

Thus, the community-owned monopolist will not achieve the maximum spread between average costs and selling price, or the highest profit combination per unit of output. By producing beyond the point of least-cost, the spread between selling price and average

**Figure 9-4. How the Black Community Monopolist Sets Prices**

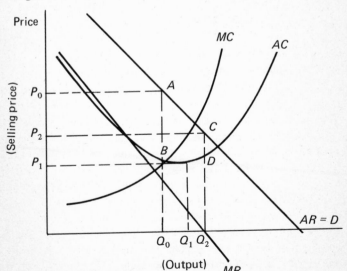

cost will be reduced, but the employment of labor will be increased. This is illustrated in Figure 9-4, where it is observed that under pure monopoly, the maximum spread between average cost and selling price would be $AB$, with output $OQ_0$, while under black community monopoly, the difference between average cost and selling price would be only $CD$.

A pure monopolist would produce $OQ_0$ output and charge $OP_0$ price, but the black community monopolist in order to employ the maximum amount of labor, would produce $OQ_2$ output and charge $OP_2$ price, as shown in Figure 9-4. Output, $Q_2$, is on the right of the perfectly competitive output, $Q_1$, for which the price is $OP_1$, assuming that under perfect competition the conditions $P = MC = MR$ will prevail. As labor is the only variable cost, the amount of labor required to produce the additional output, $Q_1Q_2$, will make additional employment of labor possible. We should bear in mind that we are operating in a labor-surplus economy with a nominal payment for the use of labor. This principle of marginal cost pricing is widely used in public utility cases, when normal profits are allowed to public utility firms.

## PRODUCT DISTRIBUTION: LABOR'S RIGHT TO THE WHOLE PRODUCT

Product distribution is represented by the factor payments resulting from the productive process. The receipt of these payments constitute personal incomes in the form of wages, interest, dividends and rent. The question is how will personal incomes be distributed in a black community system? How much will go to labor in the form of wages? Who will receive the gross business surplus of the ghetto after wages are paid? Observe from Figure 9-4 that maximization of labor inputs (to the point where marginal labor cost equals selling price) raises the wage share of the total product in the black community by increasing the employment of black labor. As to the rest of the product, which we call gross business surplus, allowances must be made for capital depreciation—the costs of capital imports that must be paid for out of labor exports. This we call the labor costs of capital. The difference between gross business surplus, after wages and the labor costs of capital, represents a net rate of return on labor converted to capital. Thus, labor in a black-owned economy has not only an economic claim to a larger share of the ghetto product in terms of maximized labor inputs, but has also a claim to the whole of the net product attributable to labor-converted capital. This is the essence of our theory of product distribution in a black-owned system of resource allocation.

The theory of ghetto labor's right to the whole of the net product of the ghetto is derived directly from our labor theory of ghetto growth in a community-owned system of black monopoly. In our theory, all producer goods are imported and paid for out of earnings from otherwise unemployed (or under-employed) black labor exported to the white community. The labor export sector is the balancing factor for general equilibrium in a black community economy. In this case, the growth rate of the ghetto economy equals the labor-export ratio divided by the incremental-labor-output ratio. And since black labor exported to white capital is equal to exported labor converted to black capital imports, which are invested in the ghetto, the labor of the black ghetto has an economic claim to the net income of ghetto capital. In a community-owned system of black monopoly, the term *labor* applies to all community residents whose income-expenditure pattern is connected directly or indirectly with the income-expenditure model of the system. And since the model postulates a circuit flow of goods and services within the ghetto market area, community residents may participate directly in the factor's market of the system or in the consumer's market of the system or both. At any rate, ghetto residents receiving income from inside or outside the system, and spending such income on ghetto-produced goods and services, would not only get these direct wage or income payments but ghetto profits as well. That is, ghetto labor would have two sources of income: (a) income from their labor resources and (b) income from community-owned capital resources. All gross business surplus, net of capital expenses, would be payable to labor in accordance with the value of their annual purchases. The effects, of course, would be to raise ghetto labor's share of the national income in an economic system of permanent income inequality and to raise, as well, the aggregate demand of the economy as a whole.

## GHETTO ECONOMIC MAINTENANCE AND GROWTH

The rate of economic development and growth of the black community, as a separate sector of business and economic activity, depends upon the annual addition to the capital resources of the community over and above the requirements for depreciation. If the rate of capital accumulation is insufficient to cover capital depreciation, the capital stock of the ghetto will show a negative investment. This is the general case of black ghettos throughout the country. All ghettos show a general rundown and rapidly deteriorating condition of capital resources, such as buildings and business facilities.

A black community system of resource control implies an economic incentive on the part of the community, based upon community receipts of profits, to reduce production costs, increase output, make provisions for capital depreciation, and increase the quantities of ghetto capital resources. Improvements in ghetto production techniques and types and size of ghetto enterprises, by means of a community-owned black monopoly, make possible a greater expansion of production within the ghetto with a given quantity of capital resources. The main basis for improvement in production techniques in the ghetto will be substantial improvements in production organization that will be equivalent to a technological change.

The process of technological change in the ghetto through changes in production organization is not self-generating or self-induced through the current pricing process in the ghetto. This is because of the general overall condition of high cost and high prices among ghetto sellers, where, under conditions of spatial monopoly and easy consumer credit, the individual seller is faced with an infinitely elastic demand curve at the prevailing monopolistic price. As long as easy credit prevails under conditions of spatial monopoly, the individual seller can sell an infinite amount at the market price. Hence, there is little or no market pressure for changes in production organization.

A system of black monopoly, based upon a community-owned holding company controlling all enterprises operating in the ghetto, could organize ghetto production in terms of optimum size firms —thereby eliminating the high cost of numerous miniscule, uneconomic business units—provide for capital depreciation, and maximize labor inputs per unit of capital in the ghetto.

As previously pointed out, the most basic and overriding problem of the ghetto economy is the inelasticity of employment and income among ghetto residents with respect to capital expansion and output in the rest of the economy. It has been shown that even under inflationary conditions, unemployment and low incomes persist in the black ghettos of America. This condition of chronic unemployment in the ghetto not only adds to inflation by restricting the available supply of labor, but it also serves as a drag on aggregate demand in central cities during more normal times. The result is that over time the ghetto sector of the economy will become poorer relative to the rest of the economy. It becomes clear then that changes in the production organization of the ghetto, together with an expansion of the ghetto production function, will not only raise the received income of the ghetto community, but will bring about a closer linkage of ghetto income and employment with the growth rate of the economy as a whole. This will give ghetto residents a larger share of the national income, reduce income inequality between black and white families and individuals, and help maintain aggregate purchasing power in urban communities during normal periods of economic growth.